A Titan of a Man

A Titan of a Man

A Coach of the Famous '71 Titans Who Inspired Generations of Young People

Paula Lonergan

PRL Publishing
Pasadena, California

A Titan of a Man
A Coach of the Famous '71 Titans
Who Inspired Generations of Young People
By Paula Lonergan

Interior and cover design concept by Paula Lonergan
Cover design consulting by Patrick McCulley
visigothan@ramenbudget.com
Interior design by Anna Huber

Published by PRL Publishing
2245 E. Colorado Boulevard
No 104 PMB 243
Pasadena, CA 91107 U.S.A.

ISBN 0-9743957-0-6
Printed in the United States of America

Dedication

For Daddy who lived and for
Mommy who knows.

Disclaimer

The purpose of this book is to educate and entertain. The author and PRL Publishing shall have neither liability nor responsibility to any person or entity with respect to any loss or damage, alleged to be caused, directly or indirectly, by the information contained in this book.

Although the author and publishers have exhaustively researched all sources to ensure the accuracy and completeness of the information contained in this book, we assume no responsibility for errors, inaccuracies, omissions, or any other inconsistency herein. Any perceived or imagined slights against people or organizations are unintentional.

Every effort has been made to trace and contact copyright holders to request permissions prior to publication. However, in some instances, this has proved to be impossible. If notified, the publisher will be pleased to rectify any omissions in the next edition of this book.

"Remember the Titans" is a Walt Disney movie. The author and publishers are not connected to Walt Disney, Inc. or its subsidiaries.

If you do not wish to be bound by the above, you may return this book to the publisher for a full refund.

Table of Contents

Preface

One bright and sunny day in June, my mom and I sorted through the sweat suits. They were stored in a bag in the hall closet at her and Daddy Doc's house. However, it was just as my mother had thought there were "no pants in the bag." She was very right for all we found were jackets.

"Well, that will suit me fine," I mumbled to myself, "I'm sure I'll be able to sell the jackets without the pants at my yard sale."

As I pulled all the jackets out of the bag, I found a sweat suit jacket near the bottom. It was red and made out of a bright, shiny material. The jacket had two blue strips down both arm sleeves. It was in pristine condition, so I tried it on. It fit!

I said to myself, "This jacket can't be sold, thrown out, or given away. This is an important part of history."

Embroidered in white on the front, right side of the jacket was the name Coach Hines. The words T.C. Williams State Champions were on the left side of the jacket. A blue helmet football with a white face mask was embroidered between the words T.C. Williams and State Champions.

This jacket was a valuable part of history that eventually found its way into the annals of Hollywood. **A Titan of a Man** explains what makes Doc Hines, the owner of this jacket, a Titan of parent, coach, teacher, and man.

Forward

George Toliver

As I think back to the first "gym" teacher I had, Paul Hines is the one I remember. The reasons are certainly many, but here are a few. As a former collegiate football player, he was an imposing figure. His face was youthful but tough. And he had a way of doing this suck thing with his teeth that made you immediately come to attention and feel guilty that you must have done something bad even though you were pretty sure you had not. He was someone I respected for the discipline he taught, for the leadership he displayed, for the firm, but fair persona, which helped mold my life skills. I recall doing 500 sit-ups one day in his P.E. class. Yes, 500 hundred sit-ups! It was really accomplished due much to the credit of Paul. Not because of the teeth suck thing, but rather the message he had delivered to me to do the best and be the best you can be.

Paul was a t-shirt and sweat shirt (Virginia State) guy with a whistle. I remember watching him as he coached a scrappy, but hard working Ralph Bunch Falcon basketball team to some wild and wonderful wins. It was obvious that he had the absolute respect and trust of the players that he coached. They played hard in every single game. Little did I know and realize at the time but he was doing much more than winning games. He was developing young men. Constantly teaching the rewards you can reap from hard work.

There was another side of Paul that impacted my memory of the early years. On several occasion I had the opportunity to see and hear him play the trumpet. The passion, energy, and fun displayed during those "concerts" was also a treat. I always felt music was the creative and fun side of him. It is so nice to hear him "hum" a song and sometimes bellow out a verse. Music was also a further representation of a more diverse package of Paul.

In a twist of fate, Buzzy (the nick-name all of his fondest friends call him) married my sister Jacqueline, and we established a new relationship as brother-in-law. He has been a wonderful husband and father. The mere fact that he has a bound manuscript written by an off spring speaks for the impact he has made on a child's life. I am proud of what he accomplished as a family man, his devotion to the T.C. Williams school family as a coach and teacher, and his impact and involvement with "Remember The Titans."

He has always greeted me with a genuinely embracing smile, a strong handshake and "what's up brother?" that has always exuded his love of life and the beauty of the day. I am honored to be asked to write a forward for someone so accomplished as Paul Hines. Be blessed Buzzy.

George Toliver is the father of two beautiful daughters. George is the Director of the Toliver Basketball Officiating School and is in his 15th year as a referee in the National Basketball Association. He is an active F.I.B.A. official and is a former collegiate basketball referee in the ACC, Metro, Colonial, Southern, Big South, ODAC and Dixie. He has conducted and participated in basketball officiating clinics in the United States and five foreign countries. He officiated in the 1994 World Championships, including the Bronze Medal Game, the 1996 Chinese Basketball Association Professional League Finals, and 1998 United States Basketball League.

Introduction

A key to attaining success in life is by developing a mind over matter (M.O.M) attitude. This is seen in the remarkable life of Coach Paul "Doc" Hines. Doc was the offensive line coach of the newly integrated 1971 T.C. Williams High School football team featured in the Disney movie "Remember the Titans."

With the help of Doc and the other coaches, the team succeeded in overcoming social barriers and personal differences. They had an undefeated season, which culminated in their winning the state championship. Furthermore, the team helped unite the community of Alexandria, Virginia. Their accomplishments were even acknowledged by the office of President Richard Nixon.

A Titan of a Man is the life story of Doc Hines as told through the eyes of his only daughter. As a coach, teacher, and father, he instilled character, courage, and determination in his players, students, and children. Many students attribute their success in life to Doc's influence as a good leader and positive role model. Alonzo Bumbry, one of Doc's students, went on to play professional baseball with the Baltimore Orioles.

Successful coaches expect practice, hard work, and unselfishness from their players. They teach the importance of loyalty and integrity to the team.

Good teachers are partners with their students in helping them to be successful in life. They know the value of education, that it is necessary to make learning an interesting challenge. They must assess their student's potential and help them blossom.

The principles and ideologies used by successful teachers and coaches can be applied in many aspects of life. Success starts with good leadership. To be a successful leader, one has to instill confidence in others and help them to fully develop their skills and abilities.

Success in life does not happen by accident. Applying the lessons embodied in the M.O.M. attitude, you will find out how they benefit your team as a whole. This is true whether your team is in the classroom, on the field, in the boardroom, or in the family circle. **A Titan of a Man** demonstrates how M.O.M., which Doc believed and taught others, can help you to be a Titan success in life.

Chapter 1

What Doesn't Kill You Will Make You Stronger

The Good 'Ole Days

Lessons for leading a successful life are incorporated in the mind over matter attitude. Doc learned those important lessons, in the 1930s and 40s, living up in Norfolk, Virginia. Now, you might call those years the 'good ole' days.' Hmmmm...the good ole' days. It brings to mind a conversation I overheard Doc and my uncle having, as they talked about the good ole' days. The discussion took place in the 1980s.

At my uncle's house, Doc and he were talking in the back of the house. It was the part of the house that overlooks the swimming pool in this suburban Norfolk neighborhood. On this day, they were in the back, telling tales and shooting the breeze about the latest gossip in Norfolk, catching up on who did what and where they went afterward. They were also discussing about the past and what life used to be like, "back in the day."

Now, Uncle George was not my real uncle for he was Doc's cousin, not brother. Since he was a lot older than I was, it didn't seem right to call him George, and Mr. Ricks was entirely too formal.

As I eased my way to the bar area where the two men were talking, I tried not to interrupt. The bar had plush, red bar stools that swiveled back and forth when you sat in them. Behind the bar was a red and black mirrored picture. The picture showed a lady in a short skirt with a tray in her hand. The words written on the mirror next to the lady were something like may I serve you a drink?

"You know, we talk about the good ole' days...," George started to say, "but when you really think about them, they really weren't all that good...they were hard times...."

"You are right about that one..." Doc responded. George should have known. He and my father had known each other since their childhood in Norfolk.

Doc said he likes to reflect on how things have changed —some for the better, and others for the worse. It seemed some days, surviving from day to day was a daunting challenge. All in all, early on, he learned when you put your mind to something and press forward, you find all the burdens and troubles won't matter as much. While coping with hardships and challenges if you say to yourself, 'I don't really mind them,' it really won't matter what the difficulties are, you'll learn to see them through.

Doc was born and raised in Campostella,[1] a suburb of Norfolk proper. Norfolk is a famous seaport town below the Mason Dixon line. It is a city, but is officially considered to be part of "the South," with southern dispositions common during those days. Segregation and discrimination were still alive and well in the 30s.

There was no high school in Campostella when Doc was in school. Every day, he was bused across the Campostella Bridge to Booker T. Washington high school.[2] Booker T. was the only high school for coloreds in the whole city of Norfolk. All the colored students from Campostella, Berkeley, and the surrounding areas were bused there.

In comparison, the white kids in the city had three schools to choose from: Gramby, Maury, and Norview. They, too, were bused to their various schools.

On the way to school, the colored kids on one bus passed by the white kids on the other bus. In those days, there were some serious racial tensions between the colored and white students.

Often, the bus carried the white kids pass the area where Doc and his fellow students were waiting for their bus. Students on the white kid's bus threw rocks at the bus taking the black kids to school. Of course, the colored kids threw rocks back. He recalled sometimes they mooned those on the opposite bus.

---

[1] *For information on the community of Campostella, see Notes section.*
[2] *For information on Booker T. Washington, see Notes section.*

Occasionally, the buses had to be stopped. The colored and white students got off and started fighting, with kicks and punches flying around furiously. The battle began on the sidewalk and poured out into the street. Perhaps, these were some of the hard times, which George was referring.

Uncle George is a big, tall man, with a big deep voice and loud laugh much like Doc's. I don't know exactly how he and Daddy are related. In life, when you look at the big picture, you find little things don't matter a whole lot. Concerning George, all I know he is family. That's all that is important to me.

Speaking of family, many times I've been told about the hard work my Grandpa Hines, Daddy's father, did in caring for his family. Grandpa was a good role model for him. His example helped Doc to learn to tolerate and cope with difficult situations and hardships, which is how he learned that if you don't mind, then it don't matter.

Let me tell you about Grandpa and Grandma Hines and how they raised Doc, his brothers, and sister. The parenting techniques Grandpa used were similar to the ones Daddy Doc eventually used with his students, as a teacher in school, and in raising my brother and me.

Chapter 2

It Takes a Village

Raising Dad

Doc is the youngest son of Isaiah and Lottie Hines. Grandpa Hines didn't have a middle name; he was just Isaiah Hines. He was born in Azouti County of Carzanti, Virginia, in 1898. He had two sisters and six brothers.

Grandpa was a strong, big man. In fact, he used to be a boxer, a bare-handed boxer, no less! He relocated to Norfolk in 1922 to find work in the big city.

Grandpa found a job first at the Smith and Douglas fertilizer plant. Grandpa worked at the fertilizer plant until he was hired at the Norfolk Naval Ship Yard in 1933.[3] Three shipyards were in the Campostella area and they employed many people in the community. He worked as a corker at the Ship Yard. Like most people who worked at the Ship Yard, he rode his bike to work daily.

---

[3] *For details on the Norfolk Navy Shipyard, see Notes section.*

Now, while Grandpa took the bike to work, his wife rode the bus to her job in the public school system. Much later she drove to work, after the family purchased its first car.

Grandpa's wife was the former Lottie Hill. She was a native of Scottlin Neck, North Carolina. Grandma Lottie already had a daughter named Ferbee. Soon after marrying, Lottie and Isaiah had three sons, Isaiah, Leland, and my daddy, Doc. The boys were pretty close in age. Uncle Leland was born in 1936, just one year before Doc. He and Doc always had an especially close relationship.

Grandpa Hines, with his wife and four children, originally lived in a rented house in Campostella. He later bought a piece of property located in Berkeley. He found out the land was located in a commercial lot, so he was not allowed to build a house there.

Finally in 1953, Grandpa Hines purchased another property and built a house at 1220 Hibie Street. It was on the corner of Hibie and Leak Street in Campostella. At that time, it only cost $12,500 to have a house built.

The rambler-styled house had two bedrooms and one bath. It was in a community surrounded by other rambler-styled homes. The house had a long front porch almost the length of the house and a full attic, just perfect for three mischievous boys to explore. Doc was a typical curious little boy.

Doc said he was about 15-years old when the construction workers were building the house. One day, he got quite curious about what the house looked like inside. He wanted to see the progress up close. So, he climbed up into the attic and fell through the plaster on the wooden ceiling. He said he fell flat on his back. When he got his breath back, he looked up to find the construction workers staring down at him. They were absolutely furious. Doc quickly got up and hightailed his behind away from the house and down the street.

Despite the little setback, the house was finally completed. The Hines family finally moved into their new Hibie Street home. The boys' older sister, Ferbee, by now, had gotten married and moved to North Carolina with her husband. So, the two bedrooms only had to accommodate the three boys and their parents. The three boys shared one room, each sleeping in their own twin bed.

Raising their three rambunctious sons was a handful, especially in those tumultuous times. Isaiah and Lottie were loving and strict disciplinarians. In addition to taking care of their children, there were other challenges beyond their control that crossed their path.

One challenge came when Pearl Harbor was attacked on December 7, 1941.[4] Doc was four years old at the time.

This was the start of war for the United States. Everyone was involved in the war efforts, including folks in the Norfolk, Virginia, area.

---

[4] *For details on Pearl Harbor, see Notes section.*

Virginia's Atlantic coast extends for hundreds of miles, and all of it needed protection in the war. Blackouts were common during those war years. There were many nights when Doc and his family had to live without lights and electricity because of the blackouts.

Another challenge for Grandpa and Grandma was in trying to feed their growing boys. To help put food on the table, they raised chickens in a chicken coop in the backyard of their home. On Sundays, Grandma went out and wrung the neck of one of the chickens. The chicken proceeded to run around the yard with no head. It flopped all over the place, spewing blood everywhere, until it finally gave up and fell over on the ground. After the chicken was dead, it was put in hot warm to remove the feathers.

Doc and his brothers greatly looked forward to Sunday dinner, when they would have a freshly killed and cooked chicken. You can imagine their great sorrow when they woke up one morning and noticed they didn't hear the cackle of the chickens. When they went to the chicken coop, they found all the chickens were dead. A weasel came in and killed them all. Now, weasels have long bodies and necks, short legs, small rounded ears, and medium to long tails. They are very active and are able to climb trees, which is why they were able to climb in the coops. They are known for preying on small animals by night, often killing more than they eat. This is why most of the bodies of the chickens were lying dead and uneaten in the coop.

Daddy and his brothers did not know much about weasels at the time. All they knew were no more fresh chicken dinners. This was a sad day in the Hines household.

Sunday still remained a special day for the family. Every Sunday, each boy dressed up in his own black suit. Each boy only had one suit. The suit was only to be worn on Sunday. The boys also spit-shined their black dress shoes. You can best believe they were looking sharp. The boys and their parents trooped to Mt. Zion Baptist church to be educated about the Lord.

Grandpa served as a Deacon at the church. The boys sang in the choir. Doc sang in his tenor voice. Doc's singing would land him on a popular TV show in future years, but we'll get to that later.

In addition to spiritual education, Doc's parents instilled in their children the importance of working hard, being honest, and respecting others. However, teaching those important qualities did not stop with their parents. In reality, all the parents in the community jointly made sure there were a lot of activities to keep their young ones busy and out of trouble.

"In those days, parenting did not begin and end with your own biological parents," Doc said. "Other parents in the community would treat you like your own parents did. They would not hold back from giving you discipline and correction if you needed it."

The parents in the Campostella community planned extracurricular activities for their children at the local recreation center. Doc and his brothers played softball and football at the center while in their preteens. Doc said Leland, his brother, was a great center fielder in baseball.

Proper conduct was a requirement when playing in the rec center games. Cursing and fighting were not acceptable.

"If two kids were found fighting," Doc said, "they had better be fighting out of the view of an adult, or else both of them would receive a spanking by the attending adult. Then you'd get another wuppin' from your parents when you got home."

For the Hines' boys, playing in the games at the local rec center opened up to them the opportunity of travel to different places. They played against kids from the nearby communities of Berkeley and Lafayette Park. One time, they even got to travel to Roanoke Rapids, North Carolina, for a baseball tournament.

Life for the boys was not always about play and sport though. They had to study and work hard in school.

Schooling outside the home for Doc and his brothers began at Richard Tucker Elementary School. Doc attended Richard Tucker until the 6th grade (it only went up to the 6th grade at the time).

Doc and his brother Leland were in the same grade in school growing up. They did not take the same class with the same teacher at the same time though. Their mother, Lottie, worked in the cafeteria of the same elementary school the boys attended. So Lottie was able to keep a close eye on the boys as they were growing up.

The cost of school lunch in those days was 20 cents. Doc said their mother, Lottie, provided all the students with generous portions of food when she served them.

Doc said the teachers didn't hesitate to tell Lottie about the antics the boys had been up to or other problems the boys had. At that time, the teachers were allowed to give you a spanking at school. Of course, you could always expect another spanking when you got home.

After finishing at Tucker, Doc attended Booker T. Washington High School during the years of 1949-55. Doc was in high school when he decided what he wanted to do with his life.

Doc said his high school coach and physical education teacher, Albert Overby, influenced him to decide to be a teacher. Doc greatly admired Mr. Overby. Mr. Overby was a role model for Doc.

Doc liked the way Mr. Overby dealt with children. He took a personal interest in them, making every one of them feel important. Upon observing his behavior, Doc knew right away what career he wanted to pursue.

This was a good decision for Doc. His early life experiences reinforced a sense of safety and security, as a result of being part of a close knit community. The obligation to maintain good sportsmanship and respect others gave him a sense of worth and self-esteem. These are qualities that would be a catalyst for successful training, coaching, and teaching. Those attributes helped Doc to be a good leader in the future.

Doc's interest in playing sports continued while in high school. He played football during his high school years. However, he was involved in other activities also. He played the trumpet in the band and sang second tenor in the choir.

During those years, Booker T. had an exceptional band. Doc traveled all over the East Coast with the band. It was a very large band. At the time, it had 22 in the horn section and 40 trumpet players.

In 1952, Doc, along with the Booker T. Band, marched in the inauguration parade for President Eisenhower in Washington, D.C. The parade started at 7 a.m. His band didn't march until 3:00 p.m. However, he said it seemed there were thousands of people in the crowd. The crowds greatly anticipated the Booker T. Band's grand performance in the parade.

Doc also participated in the Booker T. choir, as well. They, too, became well known around the country. In 1954, the choir performed on the Ed Sullivan Show. They were in the same league as the Norte Dame Glee Club, who also performed.

The Booker T. choir members were housed in the Astoria Hotel in New York. The trip was part of a tour which included performances at Princeton, Howard, and Virginia Union Universities. Needless to say, Doc's high school years were busy and exciting.

After graduating from high school in 1955, Doc attended Norfolk State[5], now Norfolk State University. He went to Norfolk State for two years on a football scholarship. Norfolk State was founded in 1935, just a little over 20 years before Doc attended. Then it was only a two-year College. He played the position of fullback at Norfolk State. He lived at home while he attended College.

After two years at Norfolk State, he transferred to Virginia State College[6] on a football scholarship and lived on the campus in Petersburg, Virginia. Doc was a well known and popular man on campus.

Doc played the position of offensive guard in football at Virginia State from 1957-59. He weighed about 218. There he blocked 300-pound linemen some being the best college football players in the country at the time. He played against players like John Baker, Roger Brown, and Johnny Sampson.

In 1958, Doc, along with other football players, were picked to be "bodyguards." Martin Luther King, Jr. came to visit the college. The players walked around and protected

---

[5] *For information on the history of Norfolk State University, see Notes section.*
[6] *For information on the history of Virginia State University, see Notes section.*

King from the crowds. On that visit, Doc had the opportunity
to meet Andrew Young as well.

In September 1959, after graduating with his class,
Doc had to finish up nine weeks of student teaching. He was
not able to do finish it before graduating because his schedule
was too full. He was sent to Maggie Walker High School in
Richmond, Virginia. There he taught Arthur Ashe, then state
tennis champion, who soon became the first black member
of the U.S. Davis Cup. Ashe later won at Wimbledon and
World Championship Tennis singles events and received top
world ranking. Doc also taught John Parker, who went on to
be a track star at the University of Michigan. Robert Booker
was one of his students who eventually became the basketball
coach at his alma mater Virginia State.

Doc fondly remembers two administrators from his
Virginia State college years. They were cafeteria worker,
Speedy Reed, and art teacher, Miss Mohammed. He said the
two of them were inseparable, while they were worked at
Virginia State.

Mr. Reed ran the whole cafeteria when Doc was in
school. He was called "Speedy" because of the way he quickly
dodged here and there to get where he needed to on campus.

Doc took a required art appreciation class taught by
Ms. Mohammed when he attended Virginia State. Doc said
Ms. Mohammed liked dark skinned people. She had a
fondness for him, being his skin was almost as black as
midnight. He took Ms. Mohammed's class on Tuesdays and
Thursdays.

Ms. Mohammed told him to wear bright colors to her class. On those days, he said he wore the loudest and most colorful outfits he could find in his closet to please his teacher.

Speedy Reed and Ms. Mohammed were still hanging together, even after retiring. Doc saw them at Virginia State University's Homecoming. You see, he was a part of the official Homecoming Day festivities. Homecoming brought generations of Virginia State "Trojans" together again.

Doc was very good at bringing people together for a good time. Let me tell you a little about the preparation for Virginia State's Homecoming and how it brought people together.

Paul "Doc" Hines in his younger years.
- photographer unknown

Chapter 3

Bridging Gaps

Homecoming

Year after year, long after graduating from Virginia State, Doc did his part in bringing the Trojan alumni back together. Months in advance of Virginia State's Homecoming game, Doc and some of his Virginia State cronies made plans and had meetings in preparation for Homecoming at the college. It took good preparation to make this endeavor a success.

The "Trojan Horse" was the name of the 37-foot rented trailer. Doc and his buddies, Von Koochie, Harper, and Tatum rented it so they'd have a place to stay the night on campus. Of these three buddies, Von Koochie was the only Virginia State alumni. Von Koochie was a music major in college, attending the same time as Doc. They were lifelong friends and enjoyed reminiscing about their college days during the Homecoming weekend. Doc's friend and fellow alumni, Harry, lived in Petersburg. They hung out at the camper with Doc all day.

Each year, Doc planned to rent a big walk-in ice freezer. He borrowed his friend Carl's red pick up truck so he could pull the generator-controlled ice freezer to the campus. One year, the ice freezer he picked up didn't have working tail lights, but he didn't know it. Doc could have gotten a ticket from the police. We pulled out on the road leaving the rental place. Then, Von Koochie, who was behind us, flagged us down. He told us the lights didn't work. Doc went back to the rental place to have them fixed. It would make us a little late getting to the college, but a potential disaster was avoided.

To reach the college, we drove through the small historical and architecturally rich city of Petersburg. As we weaved through the streets leading to the Virginia State campus, eventually we reached the black-topped empty parking lot. The lot was outside of the perimeter of the descending football field. The camper was lined up parallel to the trees in the woods nearby which gave us a nice view. It was close to the porta-potty—always an important consideration.

After parking the camper, the words rang out, "Where is the sign?"

"What sign?" Somebody yelled back.

The Trojan horse sign was the reply. The search was on for the handmade blue and pink sign and the masking tape. The tape was needed in order to attach the sign to the outside of the camper. The Trojan Horse sign was taped. It was placed high enough so all the passersby could see it, and with that the homecoming party officially began.

The trailer set up was pretty cool. As you entered the side door of the trailer, all the way in the back on the left was the one double bed. Next to the bed was the bathroom. Across from the bathroom was the closet. The sitting table had two benches with cushions on top of them. One could pull the table out. Amazingly somehow the table connected to the benches. When you put the cushions on top of the folded out table, there was the second bed for the other two guys. Doc usually slept in the bed at the back of the camper. The quarters were cramped for those grown men, but they got a kick out of it.

The menu was created long in advance. A lot of make-your-cholesterol-and-blood-pressure-rise foods were on the menu. The menu included fried chicken soaked in buttermilk, baked beans with honey and mustard, greens cooked in pork fat, spicy corn bread with jalapeno peppers, pig's feet, potato salad, deviled eggs with relish, and ribs slathered with BBQ sauce.

The set up for Homecoming started on Friday. Saturday was the Homecoming football game. A few people stopped by briefly just to touch base and give their greetings. They promised to return later in the day.

Meanwhile, there were a lot of things that needed to be done. The generator on the trailer was plugged up to the ice freezer with a very long extension cord. All the food items that needed to be refrigerated were loaded in the ice freezer. The collard greens and pig's feet needed to stay cold. You might be thinking pickled pig's feet in a jar don't need to be kept cold. These pig's feet weren't pickled. Let me tell you how Doc fixed them.

A day or two before the trip to Virginia, Doc purchased 10 packages of raw pig's feet from the meat market. Each package had four feet in it. He cooked them in a large pot of water with vinegar, bay leaf, celery, and onion. He'd let them simmer for hours, until the meat was nice and tender.

The pig's feet tasted best when you poured additional vinegar on them and ate them with a large spoonful of potato salad on the side. I ate the meat off the bone and sucked the grizzle until the bone was bare.

So the pig's feet were stored in the freezer. All the pots and dishes are organized and reorganized so everything in the freezer can be located efficiently. Food warmers, aluminum and plastic containers, large metal spoons, and the other utensils get stored in there as well. Doc didn't want anything to mysteriously disappear overnight. With everything stored away and locked up, everyone settled in for the night. I stayed in a hotel nearby with my mother.

Early Saturday morning, the preparations for breakfast began. People strolled over to the Trojan Horse. They were attracted to tantalizing smell of fried pork. Specifically, it was bacon and sausage being fried to a crisp in a cast iron skillet. Anyone and everyone were welcome to join the morning feast of bacon or sausage, eggs, and toast with butter and homemade jelly with pepper flakes. However, the pleasure of enjoying breakfast doesn't last. Soon the work of feeding lunch for the hundreds of alumni visitors started.

Daddy, the other guys, my brother and I ran around, like busy bees, to get ready for the afternoon meal. The rented chairs and tables arrived. They needed to be set up with red and white tablecloths placed across the top. Birdsong, a Virginia State alumnus who graduated in the 1930s, came with another trailer. His was even bigger than the one Doc rented. He parked his trailer parallel to Doc's, leaving just enough room between the trailers to set up the tables and chairs.

The large food warmers were assembled and lit. Food was put on the tables, along with the plastic forks and cups. The sodas, beers, and ice were added to the ice chests. Different attendees were assigned to bring various beverages and libations.

Soon, thereafter, the "fish men" arrived and set up shop. They came from North Carolina and cooked fish all afternoon for all the alumni. They cooked spots, croakers, salmon, and whatever else they brought along. They came each year and worked for free. They did so because they enjoyed participating in the festivities of the day.

The fish men had large fryers sitting on portable stoves. All day you could hear the sound of the cackling and popping as the corn-bread-meal-seasoned fish was dropped in the pan full of oil four inches deep. People lined up and waited for a piece of hot fish to finish frying. One of the men put the fish on their plate. Then, upon locating the hot sauce, they would dig into the scrumptious fried delight.

Hundreds of Virginia State alumni stopped by the famous Trojan Horse during the Homecoming weekend. There were teachers and students, from the year 1923 to the most recent graduates of the school, who joined the festivities.

The day was filled with my name being yelled out, and subsequently, being given instructions to do this or that. I loved every minute of it.

However, after a while everyone was settled in and happy, I got itchy feet and wanted to see what was happening around the campus. Doc always stayed near the camper to keep an eye on the events and visitors. My mom and I went walking around the campus to see what was going on.

As we walked along, we noticed a crowd gathered. So we walked in that direction. As we got closer, we saw some of the many sorority or fraternity groups on the campus. They performed their group's marches or dances, while singing loudly their theme song. Soro sisters or frat brothers were easy to distinguish. Each group was represented by specific colors. All the members were sure to wear their groups colors on this day. The colors made it easy to recognize fellow members.

Alumni soro greeted their younger soro sisters, including current Virginia State students. The student and the alumni exchanged a smile and said, "Hello, Soro." I sensed the feeling of camaraderie, despite the obvious age difference between the two. A generation gap was bridged, if only for a moment.

We walked back to the football field to see the Homecoming game. After paying the admission fee, we joined the large crowds headed toward their seats.

The highlight of the game was the performance of the Virginia State marching band during half-time at the game.

The band was well known for having over 100 members, year after year. The band members were organized, smooth, and rhythmic as they danced while they played their instruments. All the while they created difference shapes and figures, strutting their stuff on the football field.

The game was well into the third quarter before the whole band was completely seated in the bleachers. Their performance continued as they danced off the field and to their seats. All the fans were thoroughly entertained. Most of the time, all eyes focused intently on the band instead of the game. It was the best way to finish off a fun-filled day.

One year, Herman Boone, Doc's longtime friend and fellow coach, was nominated as the grand marshal of the Virginia State University's Trojan Homecoming game.

Herman traveled in the annual Homecoming parade through downtown Petersburg. Herman wanted Doc and my mother to ride in the parade also. However, Doc said he was too busy with the preparations for Homecoming, so he stayed at the Trojan Horse. Later, Boone made a final appearance at the big game. Boone and his wife handled the ceremonial responsibility of introducing Virginia State's first Queen and King of the new Millennium: Remey Jones and Damany Khary Mayfield.

After the Boones fulfilled their obligation connected to being grand marshall, they joined Doc in the festivities at the Trojan Horse. They celebrated with Doc and the many generations of the Virginia State Trojans in attendance.

Doc was good at bringing people together. His organization skills came in handy every year when preparing for Homecoming. Year after year, he worked hard with his friends to make Homecoming a success. The quality of perseverance paid off for him in other ways as well. To show you how that is true, let's talk about his first real job after finishing college.

Daddy Doc and I
Mattie Riddick - photographer

The Trojan Horse
Homecoming at Virginia State University Petersburg, Virginia
Paula Lonergan - photographer

Chapter 4

Perseverance Pays

Young Adulthood

After Doc finished school with a bachelor of science degree from Virginia State. He planned to be a physical education teacher. He moved back home with his parents and started applying for teaching positions. Finally, he got a job teaching at Ralph Bunche High School[7] in King George, Virginia, in 1960. That is where he relocated. In King George, he rented a two-bedroom house for $30 a month.

Ralph Bunche High School was the only black school in the small King George County. Most people lived in homes on property surrounded by acres of farmland. Many families in the community did not have a sewage system in their homes. They used a well outside their homes to retrieve water for their household needs and used outhouses for their toilet

---

[7] *For more information about Ralph Bunche, see Notes section.*

facilities. However, when Doc arrived at Ralph Bunche, the school no longer used outhouses. It had toilets with running water.

There were a few restaurants in King George at that time, along with some small mom and pop stores. There was Stuckey's on the corner of the two main highways, Rt 3 and Rte 301. Stuckey's was a small town shop, which sold knickknacks and homemade jellies and jams.

However, the best food could be found in the homes of many of the residents of King George. The most popular southern-styled home cooked meals were fried fish, mashed potatoes, corn bread, greens, and chicken and dumplings. The mention of chicken and dumpling reminds me of Grandpa's homemade chicken and dumplings. Grandpa was a great cook, and Daddy learned from his father how to cook a good Southern meal.

In preparing to make chicken and dumplings, Grandpa bought two fresh chickens from the local market, cut them up, and put them in a large stainless steel pot. Grandpa filled the pot with water. Then, he added some cut up celery stalks, onion, pepper, salt, and other seasonings. As the chicken cooked, he prepared to make the dumplings from scratch. He walked into the pantry next to the kitchen. In the pantry, there was a large white freezer on the floor and around the perimeter of the room were shelves and more shelves. It also had a small window, which looked out into the back yard. From the window you could see the clothesline and the garage, as well as the remnants of the chicken coop.

To make the dumplings, Grandpa took down from the shelf a huge metal container, with the dark letters nearly rubbed off, labeled "flour." Then after clearing off the table, he sat down with the flour, a bowl, and a rolling pin. He put some water in a cup and set it on the table as well. He spooned the flour into the bowl without even measuring. After adding a little bit of salt from the shaker, he stirred the flour and salt and gradually added water to the flour mixture. He stirred it until it was sticking to the spoon in a big lump. He put some flour on the table and dropped the sticky mixture onto the table. He kneaded the dough and added flour until the stickiness was gone. He took his rolling pin and rolled the dough until it was about two inches high. Finally, he cut out round circles of the dough using the round metal measuring cup.

When the chicken was almost done Grandpa added the dumpling biscuits to the boiling water with chicken. The dumplings floated on the top of the pot. He stirred the dumplings occasionally so they wouldn't stick together. He knew to cook them just to the point before the liquid turned floury.

Doc, no doubt, missed his father's chicken and dumplings when he moved to King George. He wouldn't have much opportunity to eat out at restaurants. Those were lean years for him, especially right after moving to King George.

In fact, Doc says when he received his first paycheck for his first month of teaching, it was only $198.00. He was quite upset. He wanted to quit his newly acquired job. In fact, he did. Then he drove to Norfolk. When he arrived there he complained to his mother about how hard he worked all month and only got basically $50 a week. However, his mother told him not to quit the job, but to hang in there. She told him, "You had to start somewhere, son."

Doc retorted, "But does that mean I have to start from the very bottom." Despite his great disappointment, she convinced Doc to return to King George. She assured him things would get better. So that is he did. He went back to King George and returned to his job. Fortunately, it was still available.

There were great benefits in Doc's sticking with his job at Ralph Bunche. At school is where he would meet his future wife. First, let me tell you about his coaching and teaching at Ralph Bunche.

Only black students attended Ralph Bunche. The black students in the whole county were bused to school, much like when Daddy was bused to school in Campostella. The buses picked up kids in one area of the county after another. The bus dropped off the younger kids at the elementary school first. Then the bus dropped the older kids at Ralph Bunche. A student might have lived less than one mile from the school. However, the time it took to pick up and drop off all the kids for the various schools, the bus trip to school took close to an hour sometimes.

Doc taught physical education for 9-12 grade and coached baseball, basketball, and track, but there was no football team at the school when he was there.

During his five year tenure at Ralph Bunche, as the head coach of the basketball team, Doc led his squad to win three championships. Due to segregation, they could only play against other black high schools in the district, which meant many times they had to travel quite a ways to reach the competing schools.

Doc had success in coaching the track team. They won two championships in the five years they were under his tutelage. While he was the head coach of the baseball, the team won one championship.

Doc had the opportunity to coach and teach the famous pro baseball player, Alonzo Bumbry, from grade 9-12, at Ralph Bunche. Bumbry was born on April 21, 1947 in Fredericksburg, Virginia. He batted left and threw right. His height was 5'8" and weight was 175 lb.

Daddy helped Bumbry develop his talent, so he could be the best he could be. Bumbry would go on to attend Virginia State, just a few years after Doc himself graduated from there.

In college, Bumbry excelled. After graduation, he got a starting position with the Baltimore Orioles, where he played 13 seasons. He is a featured athlete in the Baltimore Orioles Hall of Fame. He later had a different position with the Baltimore Orioles team. In following the footsteps of his own high school coach, he became a coach of the Orioles team.

Doc worked five years at Ralph Bunche High School, then he decided what he really wanted to do was coach football. There just seemed to be no hope for a football team being created at Ralph Bunche since the schools still remained segregated in 1965. He knew he single-handedly overnight couldn't force a change in the system. So in June 1965, he resigned from his teaching position at Ralph Bunche to pursue teaching at a school where he could also coach football.

In the meantime, there were many who nevertheless had fought and would continue to fight for integration and the removal of separate, but equal policy. Two such people were King George natives, Joseph and Margaret Toliver.

Margaret and Joseph would factor very importantly in Doc's life in the future. Margaret and Joseph would become his in-laws.

Joseph and Margaret were a part of the King George County Chapter of the National Association for the Advancement of Colored People (NAACP). The chapter was instituted in 1941. The Chapter eventually had a membership of 51 from the small town.

Joseph started off as a secretary for the chapter and then served as treasurer and president. His wife was the secretary for 29 years.

Joseph, as president of the chapter, in the 1940's he had to travel to Roanoke to be a representative at an NAACP conference. It was first time he had ever ridden a train that went through a mountain. Now, he had ridden trains before, but this was the first time he ever had been through a tunnel. He said it caught him off guard when it suddenly got dark and all he could see was the flicker of lights in the tunnel as they were going through it. As they reached the other end of the tunnel, he let out a sigh of relief when he saw the light. It was a new experience for this country boy, who in contrast to Doc had been exposed to things like these before.

Joseph married Margaret Ashton in 1940. They had five children Joseph Jr., Sis (Agatha), Jacqueline, Ramona, and George. He built the house in which they would raise all their children. However, the house would be moved and shifted a few times since they lived on a main road, which the county kept making wider and wider.

The Toliver children were raised in a strict churchgoing Baptist family. They couldn't go to dances or to the juke joints like the other kids. However, they learned respect for others and the importance of strong family values. They were raised on a farm, like their own parents, with chickens, cows, and a large garden on ten acres of property. Consequently, the children learned how to work hard, helping their parents on the homestead.

While keeping busy with the NAACP, Joseph worked in nearby Dahlgren on the military base for 30 years. Margaret worked full time caring for the children and the household. In 1955, Joseph received his calling to be a preacher. He took a correspondence course through Virginia State College to receive his degree in theology. He and his wife continued to teach his children the importance of education and God.

So that is a little information about Doc's in-laws. Let me tell you how Doc met their daughter.

Dedicated to my Son, Paul Lorenzo Hines

The Winner

1. A winner is one that will not quit
When the way is hard, and he has to sit
And say to himself. I have the right.
Not to give up, but win the fight.

2. This one thing, he surly knows
He has friends as well as foes
Can't afford to feel like he is struck out
No matter how loud failure Shout

3. That little something within a mans heart
Whispers, from your faith, never depart
Keep striving to reach the winners goal
Contribute everything, heart, mind, and Soul

4. One thing sure, you never walk alone
Because your maker, ever cares for his own
So freely he gives, if you only ask
All that you need, to finish the task

1/30/60   Lottie Hines

Letter from Lottie Hines written to her son, Paul Hines, on January 30, 1960 after receiving his first "real" paycheck.

Chapter 5

Success and Sacrifice

Work, Love, and Marriage

Doc quickly became well known at Ralph Bunche High School as the young and energetic new P.E. Teacher. He wore his hair short and wore short Docker-like pants.

Doc met Jacqueline at Ralphe Bunche soon after he arrived. She was a junior in high school when he started to work there. She was a cute, 5'5" tall girl with a nice figure. She was an avid participant in basketball, under the coaching efforts of Ruth Miller, and was very involved in other high school activities.

Doc said Mommy stuck out from all the other girls in the school. She was different and had an innocent way about herself, which attracted him to her. Most interestingly, at Mommy and Daddy's 25th wedding anniversary, he talked about his reaction when he first saw her. He said he said to himself, "That's gotta be my wife." However, upon hearing that at the anniversary party, my mother jokingly retorted, "Well, you sure didn't say anything to me at the time."

Mommy and Doc dated, while she was still in school. After graduating from high school, she attended college at Virginia State. By now, this was a few years after Doc graduated from Virginia State. The two of them maintained contact. She was a part of the AKA Sorority (Alpha Kappa Alpha) while at college.

She was almost 21 years old before her and Doc finally married. After marriage, they moved into an apartment in the southeast area of the District of Columbia.

It happens many of Doc's friends from Norfolk relocated to the Washington Metropolitan area, too. In fact, many of the boys my father played football against in the rec center moved into the same neighborhood as he did in the 60s and 70s. The old school buddies all lived either down the street or around the corner from each other in Squires Woods. Squires Wood is the name of the neighborhood where he bought his first house. His childhood friend, Ooggie (Ernest Holmes), told him about this new housing development being built in the late 1960s.

I was four years old and my brother was one when we moved into the house on Bock Road. Squires Woods was a nice suburban neighbor with the houses being of such good quality, Doc proudly says, "I have never had to replace the white siding on the house in the 30 years." The house had a similar style to many of the houses in the community, having black shutters on both sides of each of the ten windows at the front of the house and brick on the bottom half of the house.

I remember when our family bought the house, it had wood floors in the living room. When I ran through it, there was an echo. When my brother and I were young, we would color in the living room, occasionally missing the paper and marking on the wooden floors. Those marks still remaining on the floor until this day.

Soon after we moved into the house, green carpet was put on top of the wood floors and on the steps leading upstairs. The carpet was a lush green, like a perfectly kept lawn. It matched the Victorian-styled green colored couch in the room. Above the couch is this large picture drawn by a family friend. The living room was always in order, for the room was primarily used for "company."

The unfinished basement was eventually fixed up with white speckled square tile added to the floor. Brown and black striped wood boards decorated the walls on one side of the room. White wood board with stripes in various shades of orange, yellow, and blue stripes adorned the other side. Popular colors these were in the 70s.

In the basement, taped and nailed to the walls were laminated newspaper clippings, plaques, and photos. The bookshelves contained statues, photo albums, and other sports memorabilia. This collection of items tells stories about the many years Doc played and coached football, basketball, baseball, and track. These memoirs became very valuable in recollecting history.

After moving to the house on Bock Road in 1970, Doc and mom say we were what you call 'house poor.' My

brother and I didn't know it, for we always had food to eat
and a bed in which to sleep.

To supplement his income, Doc took a second job
working at a liquor store in southeast D.C. One evening, the
liquor store was held up while he was behind the cash register.
The experience was a wake up call. So much so he decided to
quit the job. That kind of thing mattered to him; he valued his
life more than making ends meet in a job where his life was
obviously threatened. He found other ways to make it
financially. He and mom became Shaklee distributors in order
to supplement his teaching income.

My mom stopped working secularly as a teacher when
my brother was born. She was quite good with the budget.
She was quite the spendthrift with her coupons, yard sale
shopping, and hand-me downs. Her hand-me-downs were
something to be longed for; she had some of the best clothes
and an impeccable taste. She had a pair of white and dark
green checkered bellbottom pants that didn't fit me until I
was in the fifth grade, but, when they did, I wore them in my
5th grade class picture with a plain colored shirt.

Something else mattered to Doc and it was an
unspoken rule for the family: we ate dinner together as a family
every day, except on rare occasions. He always presided in
offering prayer. He would start, "Heavenly Father, accept our
thanks for this and other blessings..." The prayer continued,
however, at one point he started speaking fast. Because of
that, we weren't able to understand what he said after the
word "blessings."

Additionally, another prerequisite at mealtime was my brother and I had to eat all the food on our plate. "There are starving children in Africa," my brother and I would be reminded. So we sat and played around with the squash mixed with tomatoes. We didn't want to eat it because it was sautéed in oil and had no seasoning. We moved the food back and forth around our plate trying to make it seem like the plate was less full than it really was, so we could finally leave the table.

My brother and I created other ways to get around eating the food we didn't like. One way was to put a big mouthful of food in our mouths, whether it be liver or swiss chard (a bitter green). Then, we announced we had to go to the bathroom. Once in the bathroom, we emptied our mouthful the down into the toilet.

Our parents instilled us with good moral values, despite our little antics. However, there were times when trouble seemed to come my way. Perhaps curiosity is something in the genes. I remember when my curious nature got me into a sticky situation. I found myself in a position that I regretted.

I was always taught to respect my parents and not to interrupt an adult, unless you say excuse me. As a general rule, my parents didn't have to repeat themselves more than once when giving me instructions.

The importance of listening and obeying adults was emphasized to me when I was about eight years old. This was one time when I reaped the sad consequences of my curiosity.

Later, I wished I had obeyed my parents the first time they told me to do something.

One evening at my parent's home, my parent's friends and their children was visiting with us. The adults were embroiled in an animated and heated discussion. From a child's perspective, it seemed they were ganging up on each other.

The adults told us kids to go downstairs to play in the basement. The other kids stayed in the hallway at the top of the steps. Consequently, since the other kids didn't go downstairs, I didn't either. However, unlike the other kids, I opted to remain close to the family room, where the adults sat.

As the adults talked, I was in the corner trying to keep up with the adult conversation, which kept getting louder and more boisterous to my young, unknowing ears. Finally, the adult conversation was more than I could take. So I stood up and started bawling. All the adults turned to me and asked me what was wrong. Through my tears, I said, "You'll are fighting and you're scaring me."

My parents explained that they were not fighting. They reminded me how I had been told to go downstairs with the other children. I was too upset to pay attention. As a result, the visitors gathered their children, said their good-bye greetings, and left. The attempt to console me did not work. I don't remember Doc being mad at me. My parents just put me to bed at that point. A lesson was learned the hard way. I should have listened and obeyed the first time I was told something. Also, I needed to temper my curiosity.

I learned the lesson. Well, more or less. Even later in life, I attended the school of hard knocks again. Daddy found himself at the end of a switch on many days because of his naturally stubborn nature, as we have already discussed. Stubbornness might be in the genes too. I think I received my fair share of spankings. The corporal punishment generally came by a belt, by his belt, mind you, not my own. I deserved the spankings—probably more often than not.

Most of the time when I misbehaved, my mother waited until my father came home to administer the discipline. The wait and anticipation were worse than the whipping itself, sometimes.

There was never an overwhelming feeling of fright when either came to receiving discipline. I just have the normal fear of the discipline itself. Afterward, I always wanted a hug. They gladly gave me one. Later, they had me sit with them at the kitchen table. They explained why the spanking was necessary and the reason my behavior was not acceptable.

My most memorable spanking occurred the day I skipped school with my friend. My teacher called the house to say I was not in class that day. My mother talked with me when I got home from school. I went into my room and shook in my boots, after talking to mommy. I waited for Daddy to arrive home for that's when my mother would tell him about my antics of the day.

Finally, my father arrived home. After talking a while with my mother, he came upstairs with his belt in hand. As he was beating me, I happened to look up at him. Through my own tears, I saw tears in his own eyes, streaming down his face.

My immediate reaction was one of surprise, and then one of hurt. At that moment, I realized how much I had disappointed him, so much so, it caused him to cry. I don't ever remember seeing him cry before. I was 17 years old.

Later, at the kitchen table discussion, he started off by telling me, "You know you are getting too big for me to spank now." He proceeded to tell me things that changed my thinking and my course of life. Those things remained with me. He explained to me the importance of proper decision-making and to stick with the important things.

Then he warned me, "Grown or not, if you are living under this roof, you will obey the house rules. If you chose not to, then you have to go." Now, that part of the conversation really scared me.

I believed he meant what he said. It was what I needed to hear at the time for I had been consistently getting in trouble for various teenage frolics over the years. Daddy continued, "Being you are almost grown, you will probably be on your own soon and the choices you make can either bring you up or pull you down. It's time for you to make better choices."

The conversation was enough to make me to decide to straighten up, to focus on finishing school, and to start making wiser choices. From that point on, I decided the ethics, morality, and standards taught me were the ones I wanted to keep.

After I saw my own father's tears, I realized as a parent it wasn't easy to discipline me. The discipline was for the best. I respected him for that. I know it is the same kind of respect Doc maintained for his own father.

In addition to be being corrected and disciplined, my brother and I were taught to be supportive of Daddy, in his coaching and teaching endeavors. For as long as I could remember, as a family, we attended all of the games he coached. We cheered from the sidelines for the team. We went to T.C. Williams high school football games in the fall and basketball games in the spring.

During football season, my mother, brother, and I bundled up in many layers of clothing to keep warm during the brisk fall and winter nights, along with the other coach's wives and children. It's fun to remember all those years of sitting in the stands cheering for a team I loved and my father coached. What is even more amazing is eventually, people all over the world would come to appreciate and cheer for the Titans in the same way I did for decades.

As a side story, one little incident took place at one of the football games at T.C. Williams high school in the 70s. A coach's child fell through the bleachers and onto the ground below. No harm was caused. However, the coaches arranged for nets to be placed under the bleachers, to catch any potential young fallers after that happened.

My mom, my brother and I arrived home before Daddy, after the games were over. He remained long hours with the players and coaches to review the game film and plays. Many evenings, my brother and I stayed up late in order to greet him when he walked through the door. As he put the key in the lock, we were braced for when the door open. When he came through the door, we jumped up on him and gave him a big bear hug.

Through my parent's example, I learned to value and enjoy family. I grew to appreciate opportunities to gather together with the rest of the family. In fact, I recalled having great fun watching the family interact at reunions. Let me tell you about a few events at family reunions, which stick in my mind.

Chapter 6

We are Family

Lessons Learned at Reunions

Since family is so important to Doc, he and his family hold family reunions every year since 1974. They are called the Hill-Williams reunions. My grandmother Hines, Doc's mother, was one of the four Hill sisters. The children of those four sisters started the reunions. The reason was to keep the family united and the younger generation aware and appreciative of their heritage.

There are interesting people to watch at our reunions. The family is always joyous and loud and Daddy would happily add to the noise and festivities.

The first reunion was held in Norfolk, Virginia. Norfolk remains the home base for the family. The location of the reunion changes from year to year, as different family members take on the responsibility of hosting and preparing for the reunion in their hometowns. The reunion is held generally during the Labor Day weekend. The festivities start on Friday at the hotel picked by the host family any given year.

As the family members arrive, they check into their rooms. Afterward everyone gathers in the hospitality room. It was fun and amusing to watch everyone and as the evening progressed, the conversation became livelier.

Uncle Carroll, who was not really my uncle at all, but a cousin of Daddy's, would bring what seemed like a million photo albums with pictures of past reunions. He brought pictures of the now-older generation. Uncle Carroll seems to talk fast all the time. However, he is one who knows everything and takes great pleasure in keeping everyone informed of the latest news. He graciously made a full-color brochure for Doc for his retirement. Doc, of course, was very appreciative of Carroll's kind gesture.

In the 1990s, the reunion was held in Atlanta. This was the first time the family reunion had ever been held there. Having never been to Atlanta myself, it was a trip I looked forward to taking and even flying from California to attend was not asking too much.

This was Doc's first trip to Atlanta. Many years later, he would travel to Atlanta again. But, we'll talk about that trip later.

On this particular excursion, he picked me up from National Airport (now Ronald Reagan Airport) in Virginia. There was no need to unpack my bag, for the road trip would start early the next day.

Bright and early, the next day Doc, mommy, and I piled in the car and headed west to Virginia. The drive was on a straight highway lined with trees. Their leaves were green, yet with hints of orange, red, and yellow coloring. It was nearly fall, but long before the winter cold would make the trees bare. The clear blue sky glistened, as the sun in the far distance as glared through the thick forest. What a perfect day for a road trip.

After an hour, we made a brief stop to see my grandparents in King George, Virginia. After visiting for a while, we drove another 3-1/2 hours to Norfolk, back to Doc's hometown. In Norfolk, we met up with Uncle George, my father's fleshy brother, Leland, Leland's wife, Pearl, and Aunt Velma.

I know I'm veering off, but let me tell you what I learned from Aunt Pearl at a family reunion. Now, Aunt Pearl is a straightforward kind of person. At an earlier family reunion, it was from my Aunt Pearl I learned a lesson about belly buttons. The lesson would be well taken. This is how it happened.

My mother, Aunt Pearl, and I were in the hotel lobby at our family reunion. I was in my early teens, wearing a stylish tank top and shorts. My belly button was showing. Aunt Pearl looked down at my belly button, looked me in the face totally catching me off guard, then directly as you please said, "You need to clean your belly button." I was shocked for I had never heard of such. I glanced over at my mother who was sitting in nearby in a chair. She gestured for me not to say anything.

"...You need to put some Vaseline on a cotton swab...and rub it around in your belly button...you should never have a dirty belly button...." Aunt Pearl said.

Being trained to respect my elders, I listened quietly to what she said. Later, I told Doc what Aunt Pearl told me. He laughed as he said that he certainly hadn't heard of doing either. Nevertheless, I took the counsel to heart. Ever since then I have regularly checked my belly button.

Now, let's go back to the reunion in Atlanta. On this particular road trip, it was Uncle Leland, Aunt Pearl, Uncle George, mommy, Doc, and me. Uncle George had a large white Winabago. George and Velma hopped in, while my parents, my aunt and uncle, and I piled into my uncle's car. Like a small caravan, we headed south to Atlanta.

After driving a little while, we stopped at a roadside restaurant to get some lunch since we had grown tired of the dried nuts, fruit, and juices in small cartons my mother brought along.

Then, only in my early 20s, I was working part time as a temporary secretary. Consequently, my trip to Maryland from California was accomplished on a shoe string budget. I was expecting my paycheck to be automatically deposited into my account that week, but that wouldn't happen until after we return to Maryland. Needless to say, my spending money was quite limited at this point in the trip.

Doc noted while in the restaurant everyone ordered something to eat, except mommy and me. Now, it wasn't unusual for mommy not to order food. She has never fancied restaurant food much. But for me not order seemed odd to Dad and he expressed his concern to me as we walked to the parking lot.

Outside the restaurant, he directly asked, "Do you have any money?"

"I have a little, but I'm waiting for my next check to be deposited," was my sheepish reply.

"Here take this," as he handed me a $100 bill.

Aunt Pearl, who had seen the exchange of money from his hand to mine, said something about father's being great.

My most appreciative response was, "Yes," giving him a hug at the same time.

After we freshened up in the bathroom, we got ready to roll. Suddenly, Aunt Velma spoke up and asked me if I wanted to ride with her and George.

She spotted my glance toward my mother. She asked if I didn't mind leaving my mother. Really, it wasn't my desire to leave my parents being I had come all this way just to see them. I took a second or so to decide, but, "I don't mind," was my final response. I figured it might turn out to be an interesting ride. So I jumped into the Winabago with Uncle George and Aunt Velma and we took off toward Atlanta, following Uncle Leland.

Now, Aunt Velma was a true speaker of her mind. I'm not sure how she is related to us, but everyone in the family called her Aunt Velma. She was quite vivacious despite her being in her 70s at the time, and she was kind to me. I found her delightful to be around, because she loved to talk and I loved to listen.

With money in my pocket and financial worries temporarily diminished, the rest of the trip could now be savored...and, in fact, it was. The two elders and I had deep, thought provoking conversation as we rode along. We covered the big stuff - life, the past, and, my most important subject, the Bible. As a consequence, the journey with them was very refreshing.

As the day faded into evening, we were happy to stop for the night in the small town of Lumberton, North Carolina. We started looking for a hotel to stay in because the two car groups decided they had enough of driving for the day. When a hotel was spotted along side the road, we exited the highway and drove into its parking lot.

Daddy and Uncle Leland walked toward the front office to arrange our rentals for the night. After a few minutes, the two of them walked back to the cars, talking loudly, and complaining about something. When they finally reached us, they explained what had happened.

"As it happens," Doc told us, "the front desk clerk said they didn't have any rooms available." All heads turned toward the parking lot, which was obviously not full.

The brothers, Doc and Uncle Leland, had a great time reminiscing about this during the rest of the trip. They jested about how the hotel didn't want to rent to "black folks."

Doc didn't seem to mind this little incident, in fact, he joked about it the whole trip. This was something he had experienced many times before. "As we drive further below the Mason Dixon," he said, "nothing will surprise me."

Aunt Pearl quipped next time they would have to send in the ladies, her and mommy. Apparently, those big black men, Doc and Uncle Leland, must have scared the hotel attendants.

We got back in our cars and drove a few miles further south, eventually coming to another town. There, we found a hotel that, fortunately, "had rooms available." We settled at the hotel for the night.

The next day, we drove to Atlanta. We arrived in good time, because we were one of the first family members to check into our rooms. We stayed at the Peachtree Hotel, located in the heart of the city in Downtown Atlanta.

In fact, we were by ourselves at hotel for quite a while. You're probably wondering where the rest of the family was. Let me tell you about the Peachtree first.

The Peachtree was elegant, with high ceilings and hanging chandeliers. It had a long, winding staircase, which led you to the check-in desk. A man played piano in one corner of the room in an area surrounded by plush, burgundy seats. The color of the carpet was multicolored with burgundy. It matched the furniture. I was in total awe by the beauty and luxuriousness of the hotel. I had never stayed in a hotel before as lavish and extravagant as the Peachtree. Boy, I was so glad Doc paid the hotel bill. I know it had to be expensive, even though we did get the group discount.

The hosts for this reunion were Donald and his wife, Angie. To me, they were the perfect couple. Or at least, they seemed perfect to me, and I was impressed. They organized the event very well. Angie and Donald planned the reunion to the tee.

Angie graduated from Spellman. She was a tall, attractive black woman with hair that bounced when she walked. Donald graduated from Morehouse. Donald was the one who was related by blood to the Hill-Williams clan. They had two very cute, elementary school age children, a boy and a girl. Donald, Angie, and the kids, like us, waited with us for the rest of the family to arrive.

Then, finally, several busloads of family members arrived, more than eight hours later than planned! As the exhausted family members filed out of the bus, each of them swore never to take the bus again. The next time, they would drive a car like we did.

Atlanta is a city full of history. We visited many well-known historical sites like the Underground Railroad and the Martin Luther King Center. However, as we toured through the city, sure enough, we "crossed the railroad tracks," as Doc would say. He then talked about growing up in Norfolk, a city divided by these tracks.

"Sometimes there were the literal tracks, which divided people, other times the tracks were invisible..." Doc said. The invisible tracks represented divisions, conflict-ridden feelings, and demarcation.

Daddy continued, "It seems to me every city has those tracks somehow, somewhere." Atlanta, it seemed, was no exception.

Sometimes those tracks divided race. Sometimes they divided the economically impoverished from those well-off. Sometimes the tracks exist only in people's minds. They are composed of preconceived notions and dimly recognized prejudices, which don't allow them to accept the variety and uniqueness in the world.

Doc taught me that I was neither inferior nor superior to others, but generally all people were the same. When I was four, we moved into a predominantly white neighborhood. During my early years of preschool and elementary school, most of my friends were white. In family photo albums, there are pictures of my friends and me. In some pictures I am the only little dark-skinned child surrounded by my little blond, brown, and redheaded friends.

My Caucasian friends were always welcome to my house. I frequented their houses as well. We ate, slept, and played together. I was never taught there was something wrong with associating with others who were different.

Doc grew up in a segregated society. He personally experienced hatred from others, because of racial or ethnic differences. Nevertheless, he didn't allow his experiences to negatively affect me. Subsequently, I learned not to develop bitterness toward others, because of real or imagined discrimination.

It took many years before I understood and appreciated the gift of tolerance from my parents. I learned to maintain a healthy measure of self-esteem, but not to put others down. Doc taught me the value of not prejudging others. He felt it started with the right attitude. A person must focus and exercise discipline, despite what others say or do. He believed in improving himself. I'll tell you some ways he did so personally.

Chapter 7

Honing his Craft

The Teacher Goes to School

After Doc left Ralph Bunche High School in 1965, he took a job at Pomonkey High School in Charles County, Maryland. He taught physical education and coached football for one year in this racially mixed school, until it was closed down.

Then Doc transferred to Lackey High School in Charles County, Maryland. During the summer break from coaching and teaching, he went to football seminars and camps. These camps were geared toward football coaches.

In the early 60s, Doc attended the Kodak Coach of the Year clinic. It was held at the Shorem Hotel on Calvert Street off Connecticut Avenue in Washington, D.C. The top 1,500 coaches in the nation attended. The best college and professional coaches in the country were guest speakers at the seminars.

Only a few sports clinics in the country accepted blacks. The Kodak Clinic was one that did. Doc used the mind over matter attitude in this instance. He didn't let the existence of discrimination "get under his skin." He and the other black coaches endured blatant prejudice at times. Because of this commonality, they developed close relationships. He kept in mind attendance at these seminars made it possible for him hone his skills—to become a better football coach and a successful leader.

After attending the camp, Doc maintained contact and shared game film with the other black coaches like Herman Boone, Ken Freeman, Sam Jordan and Robert Cashwell. In particular, Herman and Dad exchanged ideas on coaching, which would be beneficial in the future, as you will see.

Meanwhile, in September 1970, Doc transferred from Maryland to the Alexandria Virginia School System. He taught at Parker Gray School.[8] He was one of four blacks teaching at the predominantly white school. However, he didn't get to coach football again until the 1971-1972 school year.

At the end of the 1970-1971 school year, Parker Gray was closed. Doc transferred to George Washington High School (G.W.).[9] He went to his first teachers meeting at G.W., and the following day he was given another notice of transfer. He moved to Francis C. Hammond High School (Hammond).[10] Ultimately, he ended up teaching grades 10-12 at Hammond High School.

---

[8] *For more information about Parker Gray, see Notes section.*
[9] *For more information about George Washington High School, see Notes section.*
[10] *For more information about Francis C. Hammond High School, see Notes section.*

Many changes took place for Doc's Kodak Clinic buddy, Herman Boone, as well. Boone was a native of Rocky Mount North Carolina. Like Daddy, Boone aspired to become a teacher and coach, at a young age.

In 1958, Herman accepted his first teaching and coaching position at the I.H. Foster High School in Blackstone, Virginia. It was in Blackstone where Herman met and married his wife, Carol. In 1961, Herman returned to his home state of North Carolina to continue his coaching and teaching career. Later, he accepted a coaching position at the E.J. Hayes High School in Williamson, North Carolina.

In 1969, the Williamston, North Carolina school board informed Herman the town of Williamston was not ready for a black head coach. Herman accepted an assistant football coaching position at T.C. Williams High School (T.C.)[11] in Alexandria, Virginia, under Bill Blair.

With Herman's relocation to Virginia, this brought Doc and Herman together coaching on the same team. Many adjustments and changes had been made. Now, I'll tell you why. There was to be a great upheaval in the Alexandria school system, and the community at large.

---

[11] *For more information about T.C. Williams High School, see Notes section.*

Chapter 8

Accepting the Seeds of Change

Desegregation Comes to Town

Virginia, much like many other Southern states, had a history of segregated schools. Federal courts upheld Jim Crow laws.[12] The courts had effectively created two separate, but not equal societies. Blacks endured humiliating treatment, even into the early 1970s. The term Jim Crow was a euphemism for Negro, and later, it became a euphemism for legal segregation.

In 1954, the Brown vs. Board of Education Supreme Court ruling stated separate, but equal schooling was inherently unequal and unconstitutional.[13] So in 1959, Alexandria formally desegregated its' public school system. However, iniquities in the diversity of neighborhood populations still caused imbalances.

---

[12] *For details on the Jim Crow Laws, see Notes section.*
[13] *For details on the Brown vs. Board of Education I and II and the related Plessy vs. Ferguson court rulings, see Notes section.*

Like most southern towns, Alexandria had a school for whites and one for blacks. Parker-Gray was initially an elementary school built for blacks. It continued to serve the needs of black students, until it became a middle school in 1965 during desegregation.

G.W. High School was formed as a result of a merger of the students from Alexandria's two high schools, Alexandria High School and George Mason High School. G.W. served the needs of the white students. Hammond High School was also predominantly white.

In 1971, the Swann vs. Charolette-Mecklenburg Board of Education case was passed.[14] The city of Alexandria was under pressure to create a plan to integrate all schools. The integration had to be in proportion to the racial mix of the student population.

Before the start of the 1971-1972 school year, Alexandria adopted the K6-2-2-2 plan. This plan meant kindergarten through sixth grade students attended one school. All seventh and eighth graders attended middle school.

Ninth and tenth grade students went two years in junior high school. Finally, eleventh and twelfth graders spent their last two years in senior high school. This K6-2-2-2 plan was instituted to bring racial and economic balance to Alexandria's school system.

---

[14] *For details on the Swann vs. Charolette-Mecklenburg Board of Education case, see Notes section.*

Two high schools, G.W. and Hammond were changed to junior high schools. All of the city's freshman and sophomores were divided between them.

T.C. Williams High School (T.C.) became the only senior high school in Alexandria. The school's mascot was a Titan.[15] All the juniors and seniors in the city attended T.C. In fact, with this change, T.C. became one of the largest high schools in the nation. Doc being transferred from school to school was in preparation for putting the K6-2-2-2 plan into effect.

Integration accomplished the goal of bringing about a racial balance. This process created a problem for the football players who were from competing schools. The players were now a part of the same school, and the same team.

It took good leadership and guidance from the coaches to unify this team. Doc's mind over matter attitude helped the players to realize the changes don't really matter, if you don't mind them. He told them to tell themselves if they don't mind the change, they will cope successfully. The players learned to look for the positive in the situation. It took time and effort, as we shall see.

---

[15] *For the definition of a Titan, see Notes section.*

*Paul "Doc" Hines walking into his classroom
wearing a T.C. Williams shirt
- photographer unknown*

Chapter 9

Can We All Get Along?

Unifying the Team

With the school board's decision to integrate its school system, Herman Boone was appointed as head football coach of T.C. Boone was honored to have been selected as head coach. But, initially he turned down the job and told the superintendent he didn't want the job just because he was black. He reminded them how they hired him on the basis of his talent and the content of his character, not his race.

You see, Boone was chosen over a well-known white coach, William (Bill) Yoast. Bill Yoast had seniority and a steadfast citywide following in the Alexandria community.

The black leaders in the community came to Boone and explained how they have been fighting for years to get black teachers, coaches, and administrators. Alexandria's black community pleaded with Boone to take the head-coaching job at T.C. Ultimately, Boone decided to take the job as the head coach, albeit apprehensively.

Some in the community, very openly, showed their animosity toward Coach Boone at his being picked to be the head coach. One morning Coach Boone woke up to find a toilet full of feces on his front lawn. On other occasions, eggs and excrement were thrown at his house. There were even petitions circulated to get Boone and his family to move out their newly purchased Springfield, Virginia home.

The support of Doc, Doc being his right hand man, and others were invaluable during this trial some period. Boone thought the other coaches wouldn't work with him. But, he was wrong.

Bill Yoast grew up in Florence, Alabama. He had a desire to help young people. Initially, he aspired to be a minister. He turned to coaching and athletics instead. He was a successful and winning coach at Hammond High School, when the merger of the schools took place.

At first, Yoast was shocked when he heard about the decision to hire Boone as the head coach. Then, he got angry. He didn't know exactly to express his anger towards though.

After speaking with Boone, Yoast decided to remain on the team. He was the defensive coach at T.C. In time, Boone, Yoast, Doc, and the other coaches got better acquainted while coaching on the football field. The coaches set out to do the best job they could under the circumstances. They endeavored to get along for there were many other things to deal with in the community.

The core team of varsity coaches at T.C. consisted of Herman as head coach, overseeing the running backs and quarterback. Bill Yoast was defensive coordinator. Daddy Doc was the offensive line coach. Dennis Shaw was the defensive coach for secondary line. Glen Furman was coach of the defensive line. Ron Jones was the coach for the receivers on the offense. Three men who helped coach and scouted out opposing teams in preparation for the games were Rick Campbell, Don Futrell, and Billy Marsh.

One issue to handle came from some of the football players from Hammond. Yoast had ten starting seniors from Hammond, including star defensive end, Gerry Bertier, coming to play at T.C. One day, his players approached him with a petition saying they weren't going to play, unless he was head coach of T.C.

Yoast tore up the petition and told them it was foolishness. He knew the players were upset, like the many in the community. He told his returning seniors to focus on football and the team and they would get to play.

Even with that matter straightened out, the recently formed T.C. football program was still in a mess. When the coaches brought the players together, T.C. didn't have a unified team, they had a group of resentful and unhappy young men. The black players didn't want to work with whites from opposing schools and vice versa. Many of the players had not associated much with players of another race or culture.

The players were displeased, even hateful about have to change schools. In fact, most of the students who had to transfer to T.C. didn't want to be there for they all wanted to finish their senior year at the school they had attended for the last three years. Some of those players were stars at their old school. Upon coming to T.C., they became third string on the team. The team members, collectively and individually, developed belief systems and prejudices, which were hard to eliminate. They had to learn to rise above their long-held misconceptions.

There was the opposition from outside the team as well. The team, on top of everything else, was expected to win in a big way.

Despite the obstacles, Doc felt this year's squad had the best opportunity to be successful. He realized their first big challenge would come during the pre-season camp. Doc said he knew there would be tensions about who would play which position.

Boone, Yoast, Doc, and the other coaches rallied together to create a unified front for the team, despite all the opposition. The coaches together helped the players overcome the school rivalries and racial differences. They encouraged them to maintain the necessary focus to be successful and win.

The team played against a few integrated schools, but most of the teams they played against were all white. Would leadership of Doc and the other coaches help them to have a successful year? Still, the question remained whether the black and white players from different schools could even exist together peaceably.

Chapter 10

A Ceasefire in Gettysbury

It's Not Boot Camp

The letter, which invited the football players to try out for the team, was sent out on June 1, 1971. The players had to develop the belief they would be triumphant. This team could win all their games in the season. It was stressed no amount of mechanical ability and knowledge was of any value, unless their skill was complemented with a desire to win.

The coaches anticipated the players to be in condition when they came to opening practice. The coaches were expected to coach, but the players should maintain the physical and mental condition they brought to the team.

The right conditioning was very essential to the players. For the players, being in shape was a year-round requirement, not just during football season. Being fit included having a strong mind and body.

It was up to the individual players to take care of their physical self and maintain the proper outlook. They had to have the ambition and motivation to work diligently and stick to the training rules. There was no replacement for hard work for this team. The players had to practice as hard as they played.

Ultimately, it took willpower and guts to maintain the honor of being a member of the T.C. Williams Titans football team. Titans were leaders and champions, which is what the individual team members had to believe they would become.

During the summer of 1971, a voluntary 6-week weight-training program was initiated. During the first week the workout started off with them doing 10 minutes of warm-up, and stretching exercises. Then, they did laps, dashes, push-ups, sit-ups, and neck bridges. However, on the days the players did weight training, certain parts of the normal routine were excluded.

All the coaches maintained high expectations of the kids. They didn't allow the kids to sucker out. They held a positive and firm hold on the lives and actions of the kids they coached.

In an effort to create a sense of unity the coaches had a team meeting regularly. Each coach spoke a few words to the players.

In the first meeting, Doc only said a few brief words, to the surprise of the players. However, there was chagrin when they came to realize what he meant.

"Listen up, listen up, listen up," Doc said, "I only got one thing to say...It's mind over matter. If you don't mind what we are going to do with you, then it don't matter. Thank you."

Upon hearing Doc say that, the players then knew they would have to work hard. Doc's main focus was each of the players gave him the best effort they could give. Individually, they had to work hard and put forth effort together as a team. That's all that mattered to Doc.

In an effort to help the boys to become a cohesive unit, they attended football camp in Gettysburg, Pennsylvania from August 22-29, 1971. The maintained a strict schedule at the T.C. Williams football camp. It included three meals a day, morning and afternoon practices, team meetings, and a precise bed time of 10 p.m.

The players had to have their parent sign a permission slip. Also, the players had to sign a form in which they showed their agreement to follow the requirements and schedule at camp. Both forms had to be signed and returned to Coach Boone before the players were allowed to attend camp.

On August 22, 1971, the players had to arrive at the school on time to go to camp. After checking in, the players loaded on the buses.

Doc noticed the students loaded the buses in a way that the black players and white players were all sitting on different buses. Doc mentioned this observation to Boone. Boone made everyone get off the bus. Boone separated the players by offense and defense. He placed the offensive players on one bus and defensive players on another. Consequently, black and white players sat together.

With the players loaded on the bus, Doc told Boone he was going to ride to Gettysburg in the car with Coach Yoast. Yoast recently purchased a brand new Cadillac. Doc followed the bus from Alexandria to Gettysburg in comfort and style in Yoast's car.

The housing conditions were deliberately racially mixed in the dormitory at the college, where the football camp was held. While at camp, each player was required talk at length with his black or white roommate. He had to learn everything about him. Then he had to tell what he learned about the person to the coach assigned to him. The coaches were held responsible to make sure the players followed through on getting better acquainted.

As a little side note, Doc enjoys singing. It started when he was a youngster in the church and school choir. He loves music, singing, humming, and whistling. In fact, many times he whistled while coaching on the field. The players attempted to imitate him. Doc told them, "You'll never whistle as well as I can. This is a lifelong exercise for me."

With this love of music and singing, Doc instituted at camp what would be called the "talent show." Participating in the "talent show" became a favorite tradition. Doc led the players in a ritual of singing and dancing a song.

"We don't need no music, dah, dah, dah, dah dah. We don't need no music, dah, dah, dah, dah dah" was the chorus. As he sang the song, the players followed in a row behind him, mimicking and singing along. They marched along singing, and swinging and swaying their arms.

Mind you, during practice at camp, Jellybelly, AKA Jessie Williams, hurt his wrist. His arm was in a light cast. Because of this Jelly had not been able to practice all week.

When it came time for the talent show, Jelly forgot he was hurt. He got wrapped up in the singing and dancing with the coach and players. He started swinging his supposedly hurt arm, up and down, back and forth, marching with the other players singing, "We don't need no music, dah, dah, dah, dah dah."

All of a sudden, there was a hush in the room and everyone got silent. They turned and looked at Jelly. Everyone then realized Jelly really wasn't hurt. He must have faked it, because his arm was swaying just as much as everyone else's. Jelly has never lived that down.

The Titans developed a chant. The words were, "Everywhere we go, everywhere we go... people wanna know, people wanna know. Who we are, who we are. So we tell them, So we tell them. We are the Titans, We are the Titans. The mighty, mighty Titans, the mighty, mighty Titans....oh-ah-oh-yeah-oh-ah-oh yeah." This tune was a favorite motivating cheer for the team.

While in Gettysburg, the coaches really worked hard to really help the players to become an cohesive unit. Doc told the players, "Not everyone on a team is going to get along perfectly and be best friends. But even if you don't grow to love each other, you will respect one another."

For the most part during camp, the players learned to get along. Since they had to work so hard, they wouldn't have enough energy to thrown punches at one another or have any fights off the field. Well, there might have been a few 'pushing matches' on the field by a couple guys. It is hard to play a violent game without the occasional loss of temper. However, when disagreements arose with the players, they smoothed out their problems as they were authorized by the coaches to run a mile around the field. All 5,280 feet.

By the end of the camp, the players truly became a team. They put aside their differences from the standpoint of race, school rivalries, and positions. However, there were still some pre-game preparations to be made on and off the field before the first game of the season.

Chapter 11

Thank God Almost We're Ready at Last

Pre-Game Prep

By the first day of practice on August 16th, the line was required to be ready to run a 6-minute and 30-second mile. The backs and wide-outs had to be prepared to run a 6-minute mile. Also, all the players were required to show up for the first day of practice in order to be on the team.

One player, Jim Brown, was out of town with his family, so he was not at practice on the first day. He and his mother showed up at the field three days later to talk to Doc. His mother explained what happen and why Jim wasn't able to be at the first day of practice. Jim really wanted to play on the team.

Doc knew Herman's rule. However, he told Jim to come back later in the afternoon to meet the trainer, Herb Shriner. Herb gave Jim football equipment. Doc told Jim to just come in and start practicing. Jim did just so. Doc never told Herman what happen and Herman never noticed. So Jim played for the Titan team despite missing the first few days of practice. It was 30 years later when Herman finally found out.

Before the start of the season, Doc, the offensive line coach, noticed Dan Carl playing for the defense. Dan was 6'5" and 255 pounds. Doc wanted Dan to be on his offensive line. Doc bargained to trade Dan, for two players on the offensive line, Louie Lastik and Gerry Nichols. They weighed 225 and 235 respectively. The negotiations worked. Doc got Dan to play as an offensive tackle under his leadership on the team.

Dan Carl, Fred Alderson, Jim Brown, Jerry Buck, and Dave Stewart composed Doc's offensive line. They were known as "Doc's Hogs." The name "Hogs" was a takeoff from the name of the Washington Redskin's offensive line called "The Hogs."

The offense line was forced to work very hard under Doc. The offense typically used a seven-man blocking sled, which measures an offensive lineman's strength and technique. Most normal blocking sleds are equipped with seven players on it. However, Doc had two players pushing a seven-man blocking sled. This was done to increase their strength. The players really had to dig deep down within themselves and find the strength to move it. However, because of this, Doc's offensive line was exceptionally strong and tough.

Another exercise all the players had to do was the dreaded fourth quarter or "up-down" drills. They shuffled in place, dropped down to the ground, got back up, and continued to shuffle in place again. They did this over and over. They repeated the drills nonstop, until the coach blew his whistle. The whole time, as the players exhaustedly did the drills, Doc walked around saying, "You'll pass out before you die, so keep working." The Titans players practiced hard and the results were beneficial. They felt they could have an undefeated season. A sense of solidarity grew between the players. Such positive effects were shown on and off the field.

The football team's good will, which was initially created during camp, was infectious. At the start of the school year and the football season, the students from the old Hammond and G.W. high schools sat separately from the students at T.C. The whites sat apart from the blacks, regardless of their previous school. There was no unity.

The kids saw how well the football players were getting along, how the team members sat together. The other students eventually started sitting together, too. It wasn't a perfect situation. There were some moments of tension and stress. But, overall, good race relations were fostered between the students.

A great incentive to "keep the peace" was given by the Alexandria school board. The board made a rule if there were any fights at the opening football game, the whole football season would be canceled. No one wanted that to happen, so everyone worked hard to get along.

Occasionally, disruptions in the school came from outsiders. When interruptions occurred, the coaches told the football players to wear their jerseys. They were instructed to stand in the doorways of the exit doors in the school to keep strangers out. The players were real peacemakers in the school. Later, their influence spread beyond the walls of the school. They affected the community in the same positive way, we shall see.

Chapter 12

Reaping the Rewards

Let the Season Begin

After camp and many weeks of practice, the season began for the Titans. There was quite a bit of stress and pressure on Coach Boone. Before each game, he got sick to his stomach, due to worrying about the outcome. Most times, he wouldn't eat the whole day, for if he did the food came right back up.

Here is a bit of information regarding the Titans uniforms and the team. The original colors for T.C. were red, white and gold. However, after the merger of the three schools, the colors were changed to red, white and blue. The color red was brought from T.C. The color blue came from G.W. and the color white from Hammond.

The uniforms the football players wore at games played on their home field were white. The jerseys had red letters on the front, back, and on the top of the shoulder pads. They also had white jerseys with red stripes around the edge of the shoulder. The uniforms worn for away games were blue with numbers on the front, back, and sleeves being white.

The Titan players had an intimidating way about themselves. They displayed it as they filed out into the field to warm up before their games. They did so in a way it drew attention from everyone in the stands, including the opposition.

The defensive players came out first, including the quarterbacks, receivers, kickers, and centers. As they walked out, they pounded on each other's shoulder pads. When they did so there was a resounding noise that vibrated throughout the stadium.

A few minutes later, the offensive players came out, including the rest of the backs and linebackers. Finally, the linemen came out. All of them pounded on the shoulder pads. Lastly, the special team players filed out. When everyone was on the field, they lined up and did warm-up exercises.

Just for your information, the Titan's games back then were not televised. The first Monday night football game to be televised was between the Jets and the Browns and that wasn't until September 21, 1970. However, the Titans' games were covered in the local newspaper.

The Titan players were tough. They were composed of the best players from three high schools. The players survived camp and had practiced hard. They were ready for the season to begin.

In the first game of the season, the Titans played against Herndon High School. In the first game the Titans beat Herndon 19 to 0. The second game the Titans played was against Yorktown High School and beat them 25 to 0.

Next, the Titans played against Hayfield High School and beat them 26 to 7. The fourth game was played against Thomas Jefferson High School. Jefferson lost to the Titans 0 to 25.

So far, the Titans won four out of four games. For the most part, they were way ahead of the opposing teams.

Their fifth game was against Marshall High School. The head coach was Ed Henry. This game was the Titans' only close game.

During this game against Marshall, with only 5 minutes and 20 seconds left on the clock an amazing thing happens. Frankie Glasgoe ran 75 yards to make a touchdown. The team, coaches, and crowds went totally crazy with excitement. Coach Boone's says that he could have died right on the spot after seeing Frankie make the run. It was the clincher that helped the Titans win 21-16 against Marshall.

Doc says, "After the Titans played their fifth game of the season against Marshall, they knew they were undefeatable or at least they felt they were."

In game six, the Titans beat Groveton High School 29 to 0. In game seven, it was Madison High School who lost to the Titans 0 to 34.

Game eight was against Washington Lee High School. Washington lost 0 to 27. In game nine, the Titans beat Wakefield High School 27 to 0.

In the tenth and final game of the regular season, the Titans beat Bishop Ireton High School 26 to 8. During the regular season, the Titans averaged 319.1 yards per game. The Titan defense recorded seven shutouts in the ten games in the regular season.

The Titans moved to the next step, the regional playoff game. In the playoff game, the Titans played against Annandale. The Titans ran a total of 320 yards. In the end, they beat Annandale 28 to 0.

For the state semifinal game, the Titans teamed up to play against Woodrow Wilson High School. They were a high school from Norfolk, Virginia, Doc's hometown. Keep that fact in mind for it is important as events unfolded you'll see.

Before the game, a couple of things arose to intimidate the Titans. A few attempts were made to try to put the Titans at a disadvantage. However, through team work and a little help from others, the team rose above.

Several days before the game played against Wilson, their coach Ralph Gahagan made jest against the Titans. The joke upset Coach Boone.

As the account goes, a little dog had wandered into the Coach Gahagan's office. It curled up in his chair. Gahagan was quoted as saying did you see the tail between his legs? Must be a T.C. Williams player. Was this true or not, who knows? Nevertheless, the war of words was on.

In addition to a war of words, Coach Gahagan refused to exchange game films with Coach Boone for scouting purposes. Exchanging film was standard practice for rival high school teams, before they played against each other. Coach Gahagan was not going to do anything to help the Titans, even if it was standard practice.

After the refusal, Doc went to work. He knew a coach from his hometown of Norfolk, who he thought might have some game tapes of Wilson High. He called up his old college roommate who was able to come through for Doc. He provided five game tapes of the Wilson High School football team. Consequently, the coaches successfully scouted and prepared for playing against Wilson.

The Titans played the semifinals game of the Virginia Group AAA playoffs at Foreman Field. In the end, they turned three out of four Wilson fumbles into touchdowns. The Titans had 236 yards total offense. The final score was the Titans 36 and Woodrow Wilson 14.

After the game, Gahagan walked across the field to shake Boone's hand. However, Boone declined the handshake and told Gahagan he was going to send him a dog.

The Titans won themselves into the AAA Virginia State finals. The game was played against Andrew Lewis High School from Roanoke, Virginia. The school board rented a plane to fly the whole team to Roanoke for this last game of the season against Andrew Lewis.

Most of the players had never ridden on a plane in their lives. Some of them were scared out of their wits and shaking in their boots. A few players let out a yelp of fear when the plane left the ground. However, the 16, 17, and 18-year olds had to admit knowing they were taking a plane to the final game made them feel like real winners.

Every team member got to play in the final game against Andrew Lewis, including those who had never played a minute during the whole season. Toward the end of the game to make sure no one was left out, Coach Yoast asked if there was anyone left who had not played yet.

It was discovered Richard "Smokey" Threat had not played the whole season. He was found hiding under a bench. He was put into the game to play. Afterward, he said he felt totally beat up. However, he walked off the field that day with a big grin on his face.

In the final game of the season, Andrew Lewis was held to a total of -5 yards offense, 60 yards passing, -65 yards rushing. The score was the Titans 27 points and Andrew Lewis 0 points. The Titans played an undefeated season.

The Titans outscored their opponents 357-45 for the year. They were ruled the number one high school football team in Virginia. They also polled second place in the nation being tied with Washington High School from Tulsa, Oklahoma. The first place position went to Valdosta High School in Valdosta, Georgia.

Upon returning from Roanoke and arriving at National Airport, the Titans were simply mobbed by people. There were hundreds of excited fans, family, fellow students, and others from the community at the airport to greet the champions.

It has been said high school football did more to integrate America than the civil rights movement. Whether this is true or not, the Titans football team did help to bring the city of Alexandria together. The players got to know each other well and learned to treat one another as human beings. They showed the rest of the school it was okay to have friends and get to know people of another race or background. In turn, the students showed their parents. The whole community at large learned the lesson.

Good leadership helped the team become winners. They were successful in many ways. The lessons they learned remained with them throughout their life. Doc's often quoted statement 'mind over matter' would be repeated in their own minds again and again.

Left to right, bottom to top: Bill Yoast, Herman Boone, Paul Hines, Carol Boone, Dr. and Mrs. Suggs, me, my mother Jacqueline Hines at Bill Yoast's "Coach House"

Chapter 13

The End Is Just the Beginning

Retirement Party

Many years after celebrating success of the 1971 football team, it was the time to celebrate the end of a wonderful coaching and teaching career. Doc dedicated his life to educating young people. He decided to retire.

Doc's retirement party was held on June 30, 1999. The party consisted of a two hour lunch cruise on the Spirit of Washington, a six hundred-passenger luxury vessel. The vessel rides up and down the Potomac River, which separates Washington, D.C. and Virginia.

We gathered to celebrate Doc's retirement after 39 years of teaching—10 years in the state of Maryland and 29 years in Virginia. What an accomplishment!

Everyone was very happy to be a part of Doc's special day. His fellow teachers hosted and organized the party. We were pleased to pay $35 for the cruise to be a part of the celebration. Everyone knew when Doc is involved in an event, you are guaranteed a good time. In attendance at the function were fellow coaches and teachers, old schoolmates from his elementary, high school, and college days, friends he had known nearly all of his life, and family members from his and his mommy's side of the family.

Doc drove into the large spacious parking lot at the wharf in southwest D.C. with mommy and me. It was hard to find a parking space in the crowded lot. As we drove around and around, we saw others already walking toward the ship. Eventually, we found a parking spot and walked to the dock. Along the way, we greeted the guests who would be joining Doc for his special day.

Then all of a sudden Michael and Julie, my brother and his wife, came running toward the board. They arrived before it was to sail off. My brother drove over the speed limit to make it to the dock. Fortunately, the police didn't stop them on the way. They arrived just in time.

We had a wonderful time with all kinds of hugs, kisses and 'It's great to see you' and 'You look marvelous' greetings as we met up with one another in this reunion of sorts. It was an afternoon of good food, lots of laughter, reflection on good times and memories. And the dancing! The DJ taught us two newer versions of the Electric slide. One dance was called the "Booty Call," and we mastered it in short time. This group was plenty accustomed to 'gettin down.'

Guess who else was there? I'll tell you if you don't mind my veering off a little bit. My old boyfriend was in attendance. Well, in all honesty, he never was really my boyfriend. Oh, but he was cute! I used to have a real crush on Frank. It goes back to the year 1979. I was 11 or 12 at the time. He was, oh, maybe about 17. He was a player on the T.C. Williams Titans basketball team my father coached along with head coach Mike Hynson. Don't get me wrong, I liked the other players, too. However, I really, really liked Frank. He was tall, muscular and wore a curly five or six-inch long Afro.

Mommy, my brother and I attended nearly all the Titan's basketball games, whether they were played at home or away. I have always liked basketball, watching the players run up and down the court shooting the ball. When the Titans basketball team played, I would focus on Frank. He was the true star in my eyes.

Frank was the only former basketball player of my father's who attended the retirement party. I was proud to hear him call my brother and I, his kids, even though by then he was married and had two children of his own, a boy and a girl. He was working as a football coach for elementary school age children in Virginia. I wondered if Doc had an influence on his decision to be coach. I can only imagine it did and I was proud to see he had followed in Doc's footsteps in helping young people. It was truly great to see him after 20 years.

After the cruise the house was full of happy friends. Herman Boone, Doc's longtime friend and coaching buddy, was talking a mile a minute about him and Doc's experiences together.

Coach Boone always had something funny and interesting to say. On this special day, he said something that got the attention of the entire room. He talked about events in the past and how they had changed the course of many lives. He mentioned very soon the story would be told to the whole world. It is a story about a group of young men in early 1970s. With proper leadership and good guidance they were helped them to become successful in life. They learned the importance of respecting others. They showed tenacity, despite adversities. Let me explain in detail how this story came to the big screen.

Chapter 14

Chronicling the Successful Titans

Lights, Camera, Action

It started off with a screenwriter and author. His name is Gregory Allen Howard. Howard was born in Norfolk, Virginia, just like Doc. Howard's stepfather was a career Navy man. He and his family moved around constantly from base to base until they finally settled in Northern California.

Howard moved to Alexandria in the 1990s. When he arrived, he found the city of Alexandria was uniquely integrated. Throughout the city, there existed a strong sense of racial harmony.

Howard first heard about the winning 1971-1972 T.C. Williams Titans football team while getting a haircut in a local barbershop. He continued to question the local Alexandrians about the team. He was told this team helped to unify this city in 70s.

Howard enjoyed writing. He wrote an original screenplay on the life of Muhammad Ali, but the project fell into limbo. Howard decided to do further investigation on the T.C. Williams team. He located the former coaches and key players. He conducted in-depth interviews with everyone he could find.

Howard called Doc to make an appointment with him in order to conduct an interview. They arranged to meet at Rampart's restaurant in Alexandria at 3:00 p.m. Daddy arrived at the restaurant at 2:45 p.m. He sat down at one of the tables. He waited alone at the table until about 3:15 p.m.

Howard did not show. So Doc got in his car, drove off, crossing the Woodrow Wilson Bridge, to head back to his home in Maryland. Soon after arriving home, the phone rang. It was Howard wondering where he was.

"...I was there on time waiting for you," Doc said, "I'm a man about time."

Howard requested Doc meet him the next day at the same place. He agreed. Howard was already at the restaurant when he arrived. Finally, Howard was able to conduct his interview with him.

At their meeting, Doc told Howard about his mind over matter attitude and details about his career in connection with the '71 Titans team.

Howard wrote the full-length script. The script caught Jerry Bruckheimer's attention and he bought it. The film went into production in October 1999.

Initially, Samuel Jackson was pursued to play the pivotal role of Herman Boone in the movie. However, Herman wanted Denzel Washington to play his part. Supposedly, when Denzel read the script, he was impressed with the story about how these young kids showed bravery and honesty. He wanted to be a part of the movie. Denzel slipped in the role of coach easily for he coached kids for most of his life. So Denzel played the role of Coach Boone in the movie, even though, I've heard Boone making jests saying Denzel is not as handsome as he.

Will Patton was chosen to play Coach Yoast. Famed Baywatch star, Greg Alan Williams, was chosen to play Doc's role in the movie.

Now, with the interviews done, the script written and actors chosen, it is time for "ready, set, action." It was decided that T.C. Williams High School looked too modern to do the filming. It no longer looked like a school from the 70s era. They would have to find another place to film the movie. It meant the Titans would be taking a trip.

Jerry Bruckheimer, my brother, Michael Hines and I at the
Washington, D.C. premiere of Remember the Titans.
Daniel Lonergan - photographer

Chapter 15

The Titans Celebrate Again

Going Back in Time

The outside scenes for the movie were shot in Atlanta, Georgia. A bus trip to Atlanta was planned for the players, coaches, cheerleaders, and their families. It enabled them to be able to see in the filming of the movie take place. The bus left on November 19, 1999, from T.C. Williams High School. As the Titans arrived at the school, there was a lot of hugging and catching up taking place. Many of these players had not seen each other for many years.

Titans supporters, Barbara Giving and Sharon Boone, Coach Boone's oldest daughter, were the main ones to make the arrangements for travel. Bill Euille and other community supporters helped to sponsor this trip.

The bus left promptly at 12 midnight. During the long the bus ride, Coach Boone played music, video tapes from the 1971 games, and the video Armageddon half the night.

This happened to be Doc's and my mother's anniversary weekend. I had called Carol Boone a few days ahead of time and asked her to get a bottle of champagne for my parents. During the bus ride, Herman presented to my parent's a bottle of bubbly from me. When I sent a check for reimbursement to them, however, they tore it up. How very kind of them!!

Now, let's go back to the Titans' trip. Upon arrival at the Wyndham Garden Hotel in Atlanta, the hotel made sandwiches for the group. Meanwhile, they were getting the rooms prepared for this large group. They made the Titans feel important. And important they were.

The filming was an all day affair. It was filmed at Sprayberry High School Stadium. In Atlanta, Doc had an opportunity to meet for the first time the man would play his part in the movie, GregAlan Williams. Doc and Greg talked extensively. He says Greg did an excellent job in portraying him and was very pleased with the choice of Greg. He even admits the resemblance of the two of them is uncanny.

Several months earlier, a lady from the production studio met with Doc. She made a tape of his voice and took note of his expressions. By filming time, Greg got Doc's mannerism down pat.

Greg was happy to play the part of Doc. In a letter from Williams to me, he stated how, "...it was really an honor to portray your father...it is men like him who so often make the crucial difference in the lives of others..."

This was Doc's second tine visiting Atlanta. Again, he had the opportunity to go to the Underground Railroad and the Martin Luther King Center. He and the other Titans ate at the famous Sylvia's Soul Food restaurant.

The players and coaches took a group picture with Denzel and the other actors. This was the first of many star-studded events the Titans enjoyed. It was just the beginning of roller coaster ride into stardom. It was an opportunity to relive, reflect, and reminisce on the results of the good leadership lessons learned 30 years prior.

Chapter 16

Premiere At Last

The World Remembers the Titans

When Herman initially told Doc about a movie being made about their 1971 team, Doc didn't believe it. So he didn't tell very many people. Consequently, the mention of the movie at Doc's retirement party was a first for many in attendance, including myself. My first reaction was "what movie," proceeded by complaints about not knowing out about this earlier.

Doc reflects on how there were many similar stories that played out in the 70s like the Titans story. What an honor it was to have the Titans story chosen for a movie on the big screen. He says those years were an important time in history. The story reveals how a few dedicated coaches, as leaders, directed a group of young men successfully and through their effort it brought a community together.

Early in 2000, the movie was shown at theaters around the country as part of a test market. Although, the movie's official release wouldn't be until later in the year. The initial reviews for the movie were excellent. People said they laughed and cried as they watched it. Prior to its release, I keenly took note of people's comments as listed on various Remember the Titans web sites. With great anticipation, I waited for my opportunity to see the movie.

Disney started preparing for a premiere in celebration of its release. Fortunately, the premiere was planned at the Rose Bowl Stadium in Pasadena, California on September 23, 2000. And guess where I live—in Pasadena. Doc and mommy, the Boone family, and other Titan players with their families, were flown out to California. They arrived one day before the big premiere. They were housed at the Hilton Hotel in Pasadena, just a few miles away from the Rose Bowl.

The event started at 7 p.m. with the doors opening at 5 p.m. All were encouraged to come dressed in "Titans" colors —red and white. In the movie, the colors for the T.C. were red and white. It was a little different from the real Titan colors of red, white, and blue. However, no one seemed to mind.

Doc graciously wore a Titans-Moods shirt developed by my brother, Michael, my aunt, Ramona, and myself. On the back of the blue shirt, embroidered in white and red, it read, "We are the Titans, Remember? 1971, T.C. Williams High School, Alexandria VA."

There were movie posters flanking the press entrance to the bowl. After getting off the shuttle bus from the hotel, Doc was ushered along with the others to the back of the Bowl. Behind the Bowl were trailers lined up with news crews and cameras. Reporters would not be allowed inside to view the film. So the media was herded into the area surrounded by metal barricades. There they watched the stars arrive. There were TV and radio stations on-hand interviewing Doc and the others. After the interviewing, they each walked along the long, red carpet.

Along with family and friends, as guests of the Titans, we waited. We looked out for the players and coaches as they, one by one, walked down the red carpet. Doc came down the red carpet with his escort Todd, a Disney employee. My family and friends called out his name very excitedly. He walked toward us with Todd next to him.

After making a few exchanges, Todd led Doc and his "entourage" to the concession stand. Todd gave him a food coupon with no dollar limit to buy refreshments. All of us loaded up on popcorn, soda, nachos with cheese, and hot dogs. Then, Todd escorted us to our seats in stadium. We sat close to other Titan players and coaches. GregAlan Williams and his wife sat a few rows behind us.

Coach Boone, and his family, had known me since I was a baby. However, this was my first time meeting many of the 1971 Titans players Doc coached. In 1971, I was only four years old. I know I was in attendance at all the football games with my mom, but I was too young to remember that specific year.

Inside the stadium, there were four 100-foot movie screens. It was an awesome site. Disney invited over 50,000 high school football players, cheerleaders, parents, coaches, athletic directors, and principals from all over Southern California to see "Remember the Titans."

Before the movie started, two U.S. Air Force F-16 fighters performed a low altitude flyby. The noise from the fighter was so deafening loud, car alarms in the area were set off. Next, four Air Force pilots landed in the middle of the football field, now converted into a big movie theater.

Many well-known athletes like skater, Michelle Kwan, and others were in attendance. The crowds applauded them loudly, as they were introduced and walked across the stage set up on the field.

Soon, the lights in the stadium dimmed and a hush came over the entire stadium. It was time to show the movie. "Remember the Titans" is a feel-good movie. It makes you want to cry, cheer, and laugh. I did all of that while sitting in the seat between my parents and watching the movie.

At one point during the movie, I got so excited when Daddy Doc (GregAlan) came on the screen, I jumped up and spilled the cheese nachos in my lap. They landed all over my mother's leather shoes. She forgave me. She understood and didn't mind at all.

After the movie, Doc was escorted around the field in a car with GregAlan. Other Titans featured in the movie rode with the actors who played their characters. Daddy was seen by all in the stadium while wearing in his Titan T-shirt. We all cheered. We were very happy we were there to remember the Titans.

If you had asked the Titans in 1971-72, none of them imagined 30 years later a movie would be written about their life account and experience. Admittedly, all of those associated with the 1971 Titans team were not be featured in the movie, there were just too many people involved in the story. Even I wasn't featured even though I was there and alive. Well, granted, I was young, but I was alive.

However, everyone connected to this story, that learned the lessons taught by this experience, is important to the T.C. Williams Titans legacy. They each have a story to share, a unique version and account of what happen and how they were affected. That includes all of the players, managers, cheerleaders, coaches, students, fans and the community at large. They carry those lessons with them until this day. Those who listen, learn, and take the lessons to heart are better people for doing so. The whole world could benefit from these lessons. Let's see what the players say they learned during that unforgettable year.

Left to right: Julius Campbell, Ronnie "Sunshine" Bass, Doc,
Fred Alderson. T.C. Williams football players from the 1971
team and the coach at the premiere of Remember the Titans at
the Rose Bowl.
Daniel Lonergan - photographer

*Doc and GregAlan Williams at the filming of Remember the
Titans in Atlanta, Georgia
- photographer unknown*

Chapter 17

Where Are They Now?

What the Titans Took Home

There isn't space and time to list and mention the comments of all of the players of 1971 team. So I have just compiled a sample of a few statements. It is my privilege to share what some members of the team living in the D.C. Metropolitan area said regarding their experience from 1971-1972.

Eric Cook is a deputy police officer in Alexandria, VA. He said he learned hard work brings good consequences. He was the first person in his family to go to college, which made everyone proud. He says the year significantly changed his life. College might not have been possible had it not been for the lessons learned and the success of the team.

Bobby Luckett as the chief fire marshall of the Alexandria Fire Department says how the team developed a genuine feeling of caring for one another. Applying the feeling of caring about others to life in general has been beneficial for him.

Mike Lynch is a policeman working at George Mason University and is raising four daughters. He said the players basically just did the right thing by respecting each other, their coaches, teachers and elders and working hard. He is teaching his own children those same important lessons.

Bubba Smith works as a Security Guard at Galludet College and said he learned the importance of recognizing they were a team and unity was important.

Chris Kusseling works at the Census Bureau in Washington, D.C. He feels the exposure to diversity helped him in the long run and enables him to get along with others well.

Jessie Williams works at the Public Housing Authority in Arlington, Virginia and said there is more to life than football. However, the experiences he encountered made him strong, for he dealt with so many different extremes.

Jimmy Jones works for Matrix Technologies. He learned to allow people to be who they are and not be threatened by others. The experience helped him to develop a strong sense of self.

Charles Mitchell is a percussion teacher at the Alexandria Music Center and had the opportunity to perform with "The Boss," Bruce Springsteen. He learned determination, fortitude, and to have a thick skin, which is needed in his line of work. He had to overcome a lot and the lessons have carried over. As a music teacher when his students feel like they want to give up, he tells them I believe in mind over matter, so keep just practicing.

Terry Thompson works at Metrocall and teaches music as well. He always wanted to play football and choose to do so that year. He calls himself a walk-on. He said the coaches taught him to work for perfection, even if he couldn't get it, to keep trying. He finds himself repeating what his own coaches and teaches said and did.

Dana Grimes works at Safeway and he learned to go the extra mile, even when disagreements arose. A sense of pride was instilled in him. There was a realization even though all players were not focal spokes on the team they were there to encourage each other.

Avery Morton, the brother-in-law of Dana, works for UPS and learned to accept others who were different and treat them like brothers.

Jerry Harris as a quarterback trained and supported another quarterback, Ronnie Bass, who would eventually replace him. That showed humility and character. He works for U.S. Airways as a Payroll Executive.

Darryl Stanton was a leader then and now in his position at the Defense Logistics Agency. He learned to deal with people of different backgrounds and to respect them. He says that has carried over in his job until today.

Petey Jones works at G.W. Middle School and feels it is important to go back and work with the children today. His own daughter, Keisha, is a history teacher at the G.W. Keisha, no doubt encouraged by her father, is endeavoring to mold students in the right course.

Silas Holmes is employed at Hampton Inn as the chief maintenance engineer and learned to do what he could, do his best, and leave the rest.

Mike Hopson works at the U.S. Post Office and as a Recreation Counselor. He said he felt the experience made him a better person and taught him not to judge others.

The career choices of other players include attorneys, curators, managers, salespersons, and real estate appraisers. Additional information about players can be read at the website at www.71originaltitans.com

The Titans were successful then, and are successful now as you can see. Now that you know more about the players, let's interview Doc. See what he can tell us about his perspective on the movie and what he remembers about the Titans.

Chapter 18

Tell the Truth
Interview with Doc

Let's talk first a little bit about the movie, how accurate would you say the movie is?
About 75% accurate. The content and main thought the movie was accurate. However, there were some things that never happen.

Well, let's deal with one of those things the many people wonder about. Did Sunshine really kiss Gerry Bertier in the locker room?
Heck no. Sunshine wouldn't have even thought about something like that. That is one of the parts that didn't happen.

Another, frequently asked question is, did the team really run at 3AM to the graveyard at Gettysburg?
In the 1980s, I was head coach of T.C. Williams football team and we were at camp in Gettysburg. We did a room check one evening. A few of the players were found, let's just say they broke the rules of the camp. So I immediately made them get up at 2 am and start running in their bare feet. I was not going to tolerate such conduct.

There was no running at 3 a.m. for the 1971 team. We had practices three times a day; there was no time for running at 3 a.m. However, we did attend camp at Gettysburg College in Gettysburg, Pennsylvania for one week. We did have a tour of the battlefields on the Sunday we were at camp. But, there was no running the middle of the night.

So it was a later team who did the running in the middle of the night. Well, I bet the run sobered them up.
You better believe it.

Did the team really run six plays?
In reality, it was 12 plays for we ran them to the left and the right. They were all variations of the triple option veer. So that was definitely true.

Did the team really dance when coming out on the field?
Heck, no. Herman would not have allowed dancing. They came out on the field in three different sets, first the quarterbacks, receivers, kickers and the centers, then a few minutes later the rest of the backs and linebackers and finally the linemen would come out. When everyone was on the field they would line up and do warm-up exercises.

What do you recall about Sheryl Yoast?
Not a whole lot in real life. We never had any communication, for she was not involved with my part of the team.

I understand Sheryl didn't live to see the movie released, is it true?
Yes, Sheryl died in 1996 from a heart condition, which had gone undetected for many years.

What do you remember about Gerry Bertier?
He was a great football player. He was a leader. His leadership was by example, not necessarily by talking, but by his performance on the field. He was on the defensive side of the team and I coached offensive so we were on different sides, so to speak. I remember him being an aggressive football player who loved contact and to hit. He was a smart kid. In practice, the offense and defense would perform "go-line" plays. That is when one side would bang against the other side for three or four plays and then slack down. One day, Gerry said, 'why are we killing each other now, let's save it for the game.' So the alternate players were put in as substitutes for the regulars when doing the go-line plays.

In the movie, Gerry's girlfriend was Emma. Was that really his girlfriend's name?
I know Gerry Bertier had a girlfriend, but I don't remember her name being Emma.

Do you remember the girlfriends of any of the other players?
Well, I know a lot of the players had several girlfriends. They were the "big men" on campus so to speak.

Oh, so the guys had many girlfriends. We won't tell the girlfriends now, will we?
No, we'll keep it a secret.

What was the real relationship between Gerry and Julius? What was their impact on the team?
Once again, both of them were on defense so my close contact with them was limited. However, I know they were keys in

helping people come together and make things work. In the beginning it was not like that. It was a test for them. They had different belief systems and felt strongly about them. Eventually, they would become friends and would rally others, like many other players on the team, to become unified.

Bertier's car accident, did it happen during the season?
No, he was in the car accident the night of the football banquet after the season was completed.

Did he, in fact, die ten years later?
Yes. He died in car accident. He used his life in a positive way by being an advocate for the disabled. He even spoke in Washington in an effort to bring attention to needs of the disabled.

He won in the Special Olympics too, didn't he?
Yes, he was a winner in the shot-put.

Is Gerry Bertier's mother still alive?
Yes, she is. In fact, she attends many of the Titan events. Her name last is Agnew though, not Bertier.

When and how did you find out about the integration of the schools in Alexandria?
The decision was made during the spring of 1971 by the school board. It was in the newspapers. I was working at Parker-Gray and was moved to G.W. I was only at G.W. for one day, then relocated to Hammond. So within two days, I was at two different schools. At Hammond, there were I think only five blacks in the Physical Education department.

What was your reaction?
I worked in desegregated schools before, while teaching in Maryland. So it was not new to me.

Were there really protests on the first day the outside school after integration?
No, not that I knew.

What was the atmosphere in the 1971 team when you arrived? What changed the situation of the team to make it better?
One thing, I didn't know the team when I first got there. I didn't know any of those kids. We were new to each other. We had to develop a relationship of understanding and respect for one another, which we did.

Back to the movie, did someone really throw a rock at Coach Boone's house? How did you find out?
It wasn't a rock. It was a toilet full of feces put on his front lawn. Something like that was not highly publicized at the time. Herman might have told me. I think that is how I found out about it.

Did you ever receive any threats from others?
No.

Something about the players. You were an offensive line coach. Which of the players was your favorite?
To answer that and say a particular player would be hard. I wouldn't single out one player versus another. We were a solid unit together. I was close to many of them particularly the offensive line.

How many years did you work with Bill Yoast and Herman Boone? What do you remember from this time?
I worked with Herman from 1971-1981, so about ten years. I worked with Bill Yoast for about the same number of years. We had to mold these players into one unit. That was probably the most important thing. Kids were all coming from different schools and to get all the guys to think on the same page was the most important thing.

I know your wife is one of Jehovah's Witnesses, and so is Coach Boone's wife, Carol. I understand Titan quarterback Jerry 'Rev' Harris is one as well. Was he a Witness when in high school?
No, I think he became one a few years after graduation.

What did you do after 1971-1972?
I continued to teach. I worked as an assistant coach with Herman. Later, I became head coach of the T.C. football team for three years. Afterward, I worked several years as an assistant coach with Glen Furman. Under Coach Furman in the 1980s, the team won the state championship again. I continued to teach until I retired in 1999.

This situation and all these amazing things the Titans did were historical for the society. Did this affect you afterward or even nowadays?
It gave me an appreciation for the hard work that these kids put in to be successful. When you look at them today, the hard work has paid off because they are successful today.

When you went to the Virginia State College, what coach were you close to?
Mr. Lawson who was the head football coach at Virginia State was probably the coach I was closest.

Tell me your opinion about the actor who played you in the movie?
I think Greg Williams did an outstanding job of portraying me in the movie. I thought it was outstanding.

It's been 30 years and I know the movie has reunited the Titans in many ways. Do the coaches and players still see and hang around each other?
Yes, all of the players were invited to a premiere of the movie in Washington D.C. Many of them rented tuxedos and limos for the night. Afterward, everyone went to the ESPN Zone for good eating, good company, and fun games. Also, the Titans have a picnic yearly for everyone involved with the Titans team.

Sound like you'll have a lot of fun?
Everyone has a ball.

What are you doing now?
Since retirement, I have been taking it easy for the most part. I do travel in connection with the '71 Original Titan Foundation. As a foundation member, I give speeches at various functions in the area in order to raise money for the scholarship fund.

What does the scholarship fund do?
The foundation is nonprofit organization dedicated to helping high school students pursue post-secondary education. It provides educational support to eligible seniors from T.C. Williams High School in the form of a renewable grant for four years.

Sounds like the Titans are really involved in giving back to the community.
Yes, and it makes me proud to be a part of the organization along with the players and coaches. The players truly learned the importance of community involvement. The Foundation gave its second scholarship in 2003 to a T.C. Williams student, who happened to be a football player, although that is not a requirement.

If you had to sum up your life, how would you do so and what lesson would you pass along to others?
Mind over matter if you don't mind, then it don't matter. By maintaining that attitude and exercising a balanced viewpoint toward adversity, I feel I have been helped in many ways in my life. I enjoy happy times, good friendships, and try to stick only with the things that count. I have really lived a good life. The kind of once in a lifetime life, I wish everyone could have.

Well, maybe if they apply mind over matter they will.
Let's hope so.

Chapter 19

How to Mind What Matters

Doc Speaks

Doc summarizes his career and proudly reflects on all the members of the history making team. Doc is enjoying his retirement, like the rest of the coaches. He continues in the path of educating others to be successful to be winners. He gives speeches on good leadership, winning, and success using the mind over matter attitude. He reflects how that attitude helped him personally, as well as helped others he taught during his career of teaching and coaching. This was especially so with the 1971-72 T.C. Williams Football Team. In his own words, he discusses the team now:

"The Titans were winners and successful. More importantly, they are successful in life now. The majority of those players on the Titans team continued their education. Sixty-seven of the eighty-four players went to college and sixty-five players went on to earn a degree.

"Interestingly, only 22 players continued to played football after high school. They seemed to recognize that excelling academically would help them to be the successful in the long term. They learned the importance of giving back to the community. Many of them are involved with helping children today as they work in the school system and volunteer in recreation programs. They formed the '71 Original Titans Foundation to give scholarships to T.C. Williams' students.

"In today's world, we have a tendency to measure winning by the amount of dollars in our bank account, the size our house, or the type of car we drive. These things are important in a certain context, but they are not necessary to be a winner."

"The things needed to become a real winner in life are shown in the good lessons learned along the way in life. I'll give you some examples now.

"The Titans players learned hard work and have self-discipline, which can help one build character. The players were forced to exercise self-control when they took breaks from practice. They would only have short breaks at a time. During the break they used the octopus. The octopus was a water pitcher with a limited number of spouts. The players would be given only three minutes for all of them to get a squirt of water during the break. They couldn't touch the receptacle, nor "hog" the water. So they developed restraint and a spirit of cooperation as the three minutes were counted down. When break time was over it was back to work again.

"They also learned to put aside prejudices, not prejudge others, or allow the prejudices of others to affect them. They were helped to break down their wrong ideas. To help them do so, the players on the 71 team had to learn about each other in detail. On my offensive line, there were only a few black players. No matter what their race or background they had to learn about each other.

"They recognized the importance of community involvement. Each individual player has a part in potentially having an effect on another person's life. They learned to be positive role models for others and they took the lead in maintaining proper conduct. The players had to memorize different plays and schemes. Meanwhile, they relied on each other to develop these fully. The offensive lineman had line calls. These are calls that made on the line of scrimmage. It was necessary to understand the call in order to execute it. They got to know each other well and came to get a feeling for what other was going to do. The result was success being made on the run or play.

"They learned by putting your mind to something and not giving up, you will see the results for your perseverance. Exercising discipline and focus is needed in order to fulfill your goal. The team acquired discipline when they had to do different drills on what was called the "county fair." The county fair was six stations in which they had to practice their drills. One player would be in charge of the activities at each station. They would have to make sure all the players practiced at each of the six stations. Six guys would start the drill at the county fair. Then six more would participate until each team member completed a workout at all the stations.

"Another example of exercising discipline was seen in the up-down or the fourth quarter drills the players had to do. They would have to do these drills until the whistle was blown telling them to stop. They learned to push themselves to the limit. Those workouts helped them to be disciplined enough not to make a mistake when on the goal line ready to make a touchdown.

"They learned to do what they could to improve themselves and their abilities. They didn't let others deter them from making improvements. Setting goals was important. Of course, the goal for this team was to win. We had to prepare the kids to believe in one another and be winners. They could win and we would not allow a thought of losing to creep up into their minds.

"Cooperation is a key to getting along. They learned to embrace diversity and to communicate with one another. Communication brings about understanding and leads to tolerance. In training camp, we taught the kids we can't make them love each other, but they will respect each other. In their respecting others, self- respect was developed. They learned to be proud of their achievements and to be supportive of one another. If a player's head was bowed low because of poor performance, they learned to encourage that one to do better and to achieve a higher level next time. They reinforced to him the need to be proud about what he was able to accomplish.

"These are the attributes successful leaders teach and try to help others to develop. In my career, I have endeavored to instill in my students and players the value of working together. Know how to be part of a team, and at the same time, to know how to work independently.

"The importance of a sound performance cannot be taken for granted. It takes good preparation and a willingness to give of oneself. One must realize many sacrifices must be made in order to do anything well. With hard work comes the gift of laboring the accomplishment of being successful.

"The building of character is imperative. Character is a trait that forms the apparent individual nature of a person or thing. A good character is admirable in any field of life.

"Courage is the quality of mind that enables one to face danger and difficulties with firmness and valor. Determination calls for direction and focus, which leads the person down the path of fulfilling a goal.

"Dedication is very important. A person must be willing to sacrifice, "to pay the price" for the good of the team, whatever the makeup of the team.

"Whatever you put your mind to do, if you set your goal and reach out for it, you will accomplish it."

That is a truism in football and in life.

Chapter 20

Remembering Doc

"71 Titan" Player Tribute

...Coach Hines, showed us all that when you set goals as a team that differences were non existent, everyone had their part to do no matter who they were. It was a pleasure for me to make your Dad's job a little harder everyday during practice by making so many tackles (LOL). **Lewie Lastik**

Coach, thanks to you and your well-coached offensive line, I never had so much as a scratch while playing at TC Williams for two years. Conversely, while at South Carolina behind someone else's line, I tore a hamstring, tore ligaments in my knee, busted a bersal sack in my elbow, sprained my collar bone, and dislocated my pinky too many times to count. I think that speaks volumes on your coaching ability and for that I thank you. **Ronny Bass "Sunshine"**

Through deed and word you have taught so many and I want to say thank you for all you taught me ... it truly became part of who I am. That experience inspires me to strive for that type of relationship with those I mentor today. **Tom Lewis**

...Coach, always demanded the best from his people and while he was teaching you about the game of football he was preparing you for the game of life. No matter what your profession is and no matter what you are supposed to do, do it to the best of your ability. No matter if what you are doing the wrong the thing, still do it right. The saying I recall him using was hit somebody even if it was wrong the person. Get in the game and play don't sit on the sideline and watch it go by. For me the same applies in work. Get in there and do something, either you are part of solution or part of the problem. Being part of the solution you are playing the game and right or wrong you trying to make the play. Being part of the problem you are hitting nobody at all and you are watching everything else go by. Simple yet very effective. **Bobby Luckett**

If I had to think of one thing that sticks out about your Dad, it would have to be the fact that you always know where you stand with him. He has a rare quality that everyone does not have, he will always be honest and truthful about his feelings but somehow make you feel encouraged as opposed to tearing down your spirit. I'm sure he can do just the opposite when he wants to but fortunately that is not my experience with him. He has always been the same person from the day I first met him in 1971, to the last time I saw him a couple of weeks ago. He's a rare bird, as they say. I consider it an honor to know him and to be known by him. **Terry Thompson**

...My dad brought me to TCW to join the team. I was a transfer from Fairfax County (the week before school started) & I had missed the camp. I didn't know <u>anything</u> about the merging of the schools or the coaching situation or the <u>enormous</u> team. We met Boone & Hines in the locker room one afternoon. My dad was bragging about me — "been playing since 7 years old, team captain, starts both ways, blah blah blah." Coach asked "What positions do you play?" I confidently replied "Linebacker and Offensive Guard!" So both coaches fell silent. I'm sure they were thinking of the POWER linebackers - Bertier, Barker & others - as they looked at my 165 pound frame.

Finally, Hines quietly said, "We needs guards." (I'll never forget that - I remember it vividly.)

It was only much later that I appreciated what he did. He did <u>not</u> say "what r you, crazy? teeny little guy like you gonna play linebacker???" He did <u>not</u> say, "listen here, hot shot - we got 85 guys on this ball club & no one's playin both ways." He did <u>not</u> say, "since you missed camp you can't join this team."

He said "We needs guards."

He said "we need you" even though he probably really didn't. He must have realized how important playing football was to <u>me</u> even though the team would certainly do OK without me. He made me feel I was welcome and needed and I could contribute.

He became the <u>best coach I ever had.</u> (And from 7 years old through college, that's a lot of coaches.) **Mike Lynch**

...The biggest lesson I learned from him is how to follow. ... but he was always [Herman's] loyal assistant when he faced us. Not an easy task for somebody who had his own ideas of how things should be done. **Fred Alderson**

I don't believe that I have ever seen him "down" about anything. He doesn't appear to worry or complain. He can be counted on to provide some uplift in any situation, no matter how bleak. I believe that because of this personality characteristic he is universally liked and admired. **Rufus Littlejohn**

Your Father did something for Me that I have carried All thru My life....Never Give Up on Someone when You love them ...when the season started I was first string ...because of Your Father...then We would play the game and at Monday practice I was fourth string ..that pattern went on for 4 games!!! 1st string game day 4th string next practice...made Me really think ...Always..There was Your Father.....booming voice bellowing TO Me not AT Me ....I would turn and see the love in His eyes ....seeing the Faith He had in Me ...is was pretty awesome for a 17 year old kid....I remember it like it was yesterday....I really remember the Marshall game....before the game you Father looked at Me as I walked by ...and said ...WHoooooooooaaaaaaaaa Dan Carrrrrl Come here son ....I walked to Him and He looked at Me with those eyes of His and said.....Damnnnnnnnnnnnnnnnnn son how much do you weigh?......dunno coach..... Step up on that scale ...well I stepped up and His expression when He saw My weight in full gear...(265lbs)......whewwwwwwwwwwwwww son aint nobody gonna stop you ...He slapped My shoulder and grabbed

Me looked deep into My eyes and said........Now Make Me Proud ...I was never 4th string again after a game ...Jerry Buck and I thru the winning block to spring Frankie Glascoe for the touchdown...and We beat Marshall...I Love Your Father like His is My Own Father ....I remember Your Father and Mine after semi-state when I got hurt but then ...smiles softly ....that's another story Dan Carl who had the honor of playing for the best damn coach and man I have ever met. Sorry for the length but there are so many things He taught Me I could write a small book .... **Dan Carl**

Chapter 21

Others Remember Doc, Too

Words from Students, Friends, and Family

Congratulations on all of your many accomplishments, and on being the best father, provider, teacher, and role model you could be. I promise I will try to do my best to carry on the good Hines name and family tradition. Love your son — **Michael Hines**

I've thought about you…often over the years…. [You] had a very profound affect on my life….After 30 years it is good to find you. You had a profound effect on my life, as you have with many others. I often reflect back to athletics at Pomonkey and remember how much fun we had, not to mention life's lessons….**Duane Booth**

...You were my 10th grade PE teacher, and you cracked me up daily. I was just this little pip-squeak cheerleader, and you pushed me to my limits, while making me laugh. Glad to see you haven't changed too much since 1984! **Lisa Buckmaster (Ward)**

I am a great fan of your father. He was my football offensive line coach during his first and second year at T.C. (Williams High School) I was the starting center that very first game...Those two years playing for your father served me well later in life. I often remembered him looking at us and saying "If you don't mind...... it don't matter" as we worked our butts off. In all seriousness, it was his mannerisms, his quotes, his general example that I reflected on as I matured as an adult. Through various jobs, the Navy, engineer, I often tell stories of those football practices with your father. I owe your father a great deal. He still encourages me on even after all this time. -**Tom Lewis**

... [Doc] you really had a hand in the way I live my life...**Sid Ellis**

#	Last Name HT WT	First YR	Nickname	P
10	Harris 5-9 155	Jerry 11		QB
11	Hopson 6-0 148	Derrick 12	Sugar Babe	DB
11	Sanders 5-7 130	Wayne 10	Hard Rock	TB
12	Bass 5-11 158	Ron 11		QB
14	Reynolds 5-11 156	Rusty 12		P
15	Avila 5-10 176	Richard 11		QB
16	Billingsly 5-6 146	Steve 11		WO
20	Davis 5-11 156	Lee Roy 11	Monk	DB
21	Morton 5-5 132	Avery 11		DB
22	Grimes 5-7 137	Robert 12		WO
23	Robinson 5-10 137	Warren 12		WO
24	Stover 5-10 154	Wayne 12		DB
25	Mitchell 6-0 146	Charlie 11		TB
26	Clemmons 6-0 163	Joe 12		DB

#	Last Name HT WT	First YR	Nickname	P
27	Huffman	Larry		DB
	5-9 144	12		
28	Nelson	William		WO
	5-10 156	11		
30	Clemmons	Henry		DB
	6-0 151	12		
31	Grimes	Dana		TB
	5-6 149	11		
32	Castro	Henry		FB
	5-8 173	12		
33	Morris	Tim		LB
	5-7 150	12		
34	Cook	Earl		DB
	6-0 164	11		
35	Casey	Charles		FB
	6-0 162	12		
36	Leber	John		FB
	5-8 166	11		
37	Jessie	David		DB
	5-10 144	12		
38	Freeman	Jasper		DB
	5-5 132	11		
40	Jones	Tom	Petey	LB
	5-7 160	12		
41	Glascoe	Frankie		TB
	5-5 143	12		
42	Bertier	Gerry		LB
	6-1 192	12		

#	Last Name HT WT	First YR	Nickname	P
43	Arrington 5-8 185	Collin 12	Patches	FB
44	Barker 6-2 195	Kirk 12		LB
45	Frank 5-10 152	Randy 11		TB
46	Morgan 5-10 159	Woody 10		WO
47	McBride 5-10 171	William 11		LB
50	Luckett 5-9 171	Robert 12		OL
51	Williams 5-10 162	Ricky 12		LB
52	Handback 6-1 196	Bob 10		LB
53	Barber 5-8 185	James 12		C
54	Lynch 5-10 165	Mike 11		G
55	Lewis 5-11 178	Tom 11		C
56	Brown 6-1 200	Jim 12		C
57	Owen 5-4 133	Wally 11		LB
60	Phillips 5-11 181	Randy 12		G

#	Last Name HT WT	First YR	Nickname	P
61	Jones 6-1 192	Jimmy 11	Catfish	LB
62	Littlejohn 5-9 156	Rufus 11		LB
63	Dombrosky 5-11 176	Ray 12		G
64	Buck 5-8 195	Jerry 12		G
65	Kusseling 5-10 173	Chris 12		LB
66	Beeding 5-11 177	Ford 11		G
67	Brossius 5-10 192	David 12		OT
68	Stewart 5-11 194	David 12		G
69	Williams 5-11 162	Doug 11		G
70	Nichols 6-0 212	Gary 12		DT
70	Burgess 6-1 212	Darnell 12		DT
71	Holmes 5-11 195	Silas 12		DT
72	Carl 6-3 221	Dan 12		OT
73	Lastik 6-1 239	Lewie 12		DT

| # | Last Name | First | Nickname | P |
	HT WT	YR		
74	Murphy	Jerome		LB
	5-9 179	12		
75	Alderson	Fred		OT
	5-10 192	11		
76	Grayson	Richard		OT
	6-0 202	12		
77	Lundin	Kerry		OT
	6-0 198	11		
78	Freeman	Kenny		K
	6-1 226	11		
79	Williams	Jessie	Jellie	OE
	5-9 222	11		
80	Stanton	Darryl	Blue	OE
	5-9 162	11		
81	Campbell	Julius	Big Ju	DE
	6-1 220	11		
82	Smith	Brad	Bubba	OE
	6-2 195	11		
83	Hilton	Wayne	Wool	DE
	6-1 185	11		
83	Ladner	Dale		E
	6-1 155	11		
84	Hopson	Michael		OE
	6-2 196	10		
85	Alexander	Derrick	Duck	DE
	6-0 184	11		
86	Harrington	Dennis		OE
	5-8 146	12		

#	Last Name HT	WT	First YR	Nickname	P
87	Robinson		Robert		DE
	5-9	158	12		
88	Guild		Steve		OE
	6-1	196	12		
96	Thompson		Terry		DE
	5-9	195	11		
89	McCracken		Tom		OE
	5-11	157	11		
90	Watson Reggie				DE
	6-0	178	11		
95	Hooks		Anthony		DT
	5-9	195	11		
99	Threat		Richard		DT
	6-0	199	11		

Coaches
Herman Boone
Glenn Furman
Paul Hines
Ron Jones
Dennis Shaw
Bill Yoast

Managers
DeBora Craven
Jim Plant
Fred Rauch

Cheerleaders
Adriane Bibb
Marilyn Buckner (Martin)
MJ Burlin (Hayden)
Lillie Brown
Ethel Cook (Ferguson)
Debbie Clayton
Marjy Dedrick
Maria Johnson (Turner)
Linda Lewis
Nancy Musser (Cody)
Nancy Reid
Terrie Smith (Caulsey)

Notes

1 Campostella

The Campostella neighborhood traces its roots to Captain Fred Wilson of Norfolk County. During the Civil War, Wilson organized a company of soldiers and built a camp for them on his land, naming it Camp Stella after his oldest daughter. After his death, the property was sold to developers, who added an "o" to the name and surveyed the land as the Campostella Land Company, telling prospective buyers that the area was named for a place in Italy meaning "starlit field".

Captain Wilson built a toll bridge to his property in 1872, and this would become the first Campostella Bridge, rebuilt in 1894 and strengthened around 1900 to accommodate streetcars serving the growing suburb. During World War I the bridge was commandeered by the War Department and its draw was chained open to accommodate ships on the Elizabeth River.

Campostella was annexed to the city in 1923 and a new bridge was built, but the congestion of traffic on its two lanes necessitated the construction in 1935 of a four-lane concrete and steel structure, built with $400,000 from a WPA highway grant and $170,000 of city revenue from bus fares and Norfolk's share of the state gasoline tax. The draw span from the 1923 bridge was taken apart and sent to Pulaski County to replace the New River ferry. The VIRGINIAN-PILOT predicted "there will be people in the hills who will feel a pang at the passing of their ferry, but they will soon come to regard the transplanted Campostella span as we here look upon its successor - as a major public improvement and a real contribution to progress". Today's six-lane span opened in 1987.

2 Booker T. Washington High School

Booker T. Washington High School in Norfolk, Virginia dates back to April of 1911, when the Norfolk School Board agreed to endorse one year of high school learning in connection with elementary school at John T. West School. In 1912, a second year was added and, in 1913, a third year was included. In May of 1914, the State Board of Education endorsed the high school and the local board passed as act which gave Virginia its first accredited public high school for Negroes.

The following year saw such raid growth that the board was forced to move to the high school site on Princess Anne Road. This site was officially occupied in 1917 and its name was immediately changed to Booker T. Washington High School. In 1924, keeping pace with its own rapid growth, a new and then modern Booker T. Washington High School opened on Virginia Beach Boulevard with a student body of 1750 in grades 7 - 12 and a faculty of 63 teachers.

During the 1920's and 1930's under the leadership of Mr. Winston Douglas, Booker T. Washington rose to new heights of glory, earning the name "The Mighty Booker T" and the "Fighting Bookers." In 1961, Mr. Albert Preston took the helm and guided Booker T. Washington High School through many major social, economic and educational changes with unaltered determination and quiet dignity.

In September of 1974, a new era began for Booker T. Washington High School. A modern eight million dollar plant was opened. The formal dedication was on Sunday, February 9th, 1975. Dr. Thomas Newby was appointed principal in

December, 1977. Under his leadership, Booker T. Washington continued its quest for excellence and service to the community. When Dr. Newby retired in 1994, Mr. Joel R. Wagner became principal. The school has served the community, the state, and the nation for over 89 years.

3 Norfolk Navy Shipyard

On November 1, 1767 Andrew Sprowle, a merchant and ship owner, established the Gosport Shipyard on the western shore of the Elizabeth River under the British flag. The shipyard developed and prospered as both a naval and merchant shipyard. When the American Revolution began in 1775, Sprowle chose to remain loyal to the Crown and fled the area aboard the Royal Governor's flagship. All his properties were confiscated by the Colony of Virginia. While being operated by Virginia, in 1779, the shipyard was burned by the British.

This former colonial shipyard became the Navy's nucleus in the Hampton Roads area where the largest naval base in the world has developed. The Norfolk Naval Shipyard is the U.S. Navy's oldest shipyard and actually predates the United States Navy Department by 31 years. The largest shipyard on the East Coast. Known for most of its first century as "Gosport", it was renamed "Norfolk" in 1862 after the largest city in the area. It has never borne the name of its home city of Portsmouth.

During its more than 230 years, the Norfolk Naval Shipyard has assisted the nation in winning nine major wars, putting an end to piracy, sending the Great White Fleet around the world, scientifically exploring the Pacific, and opening Japan to American trade.

Built here in 1794-99 was the U.S. Frigate USS CHESAPEAKE, a sister ship of the USS CONSTITUTION and one of the first six ships to be built for the U.S. Navy after the Revolution. One hundred more ships slid down the ways here before the yard completed its last ship, a wooden minesweeper, in 1953.

The first dry dock in the western hemisphere opened here on June 17, 1833 by hosting the 74-gun ship-of-the-line USS DELAWARE. Dry Dock 1, now a national historic landmark, is still in use.

It was in this yard that the partly burned steam frigate USS MERRIMACK was converted by the Confederates into the CSS VIRGINIA. In March 1862, world wide attention focused on the battles between the VIRGINIA and the wooden Union ships USS CONGRESS and USS CUMBERLAND and the federal ironclad USS MONITOR. The battles in Hampton Roads spurred changes in naval technology around the world.

USS TEXAS, first U.S. naval battleship to be commissioned, was built here in 1889-92 as was USS RALEIGH the first modern cruiser completely built by the government.

Flying from the first flight deck built on a ship, by the Norfolk Naval Shipyard, Eugene B. Ely took off from USS BIRMINGHAM (CS-2) in Hampton Roads on November 14, 1910. Scheduled to land at NNSY, he touched down instead in Norfolk.

The first aircraft carrier in the U.S. Navy's history, the USS LANGLEY was converted here between 1919 and 1922 from the collier USS JUPITER.

The yard's employment peak of nearly 43,000 workers was reached during World War II when the yard built nearly 30 major vessels and repaired 6,850 U.S. and Allied ships. It also built 20 tank landing ships and 50 medium landing craft. During the three years of the Korean War, the shipyard completed work on more than 1,250 naval vessels and built two wooden minesweepers.

The shipyard attained nuclear technology capability in the early part of 1965 when USS SKATE (SSN-578) became the first modern submarine to undergo a major overhaul here.

Shipyarders here have built a tradition of professional leadership through hard work and technological innovation. As sailing ships yielded to steam-powered ironclads, they learned new skills. From the early experiments with Polaris missiles to the latest installation of complex weapons systems, shipyarders have come up with productive ways to get their jobs done. That is why today Norfolk Naval Shipyard's ability to repair and overhaul ships with speed and efficiency has earned it numerous awards and the reputation of being the nation's number one shipyard.

4 Pearl Harbor

On Sunday, December 7, 1941, naval aviation forces of the Empire of Japan attacked the United States Pacific Fleet center at Pearl Harbor, Hawaii. It was called a Day of Infamy by President Roosevelt.

5 Norfolk State University

Norfolk State College was founded in 1935. At this founding, it was named the Norfolk Unit of Virginia Union University. In 1942, the College became the independent Norfolk Polytechnic College. Two years later an Act of the Virginia Legislature mandated that it become a part of Virginia State College. In 1956, another Act of the Legislature enabled the Institution to offer its first Bachelor's degree. The College was separated from Virginia State College and became fully independent in 1969. Subsequent legislative acts designated the institution as a University and authorized the granting of graduate degrees. In 1979, University status was attained at Norfolk State.

6 Virginia State University

Virginia State University was founded on March 6, 1882, when the legislature passed a bill to charter the Virginia Normal and Collegiate Institute. The bill was sponsored by Delegate Alfred W. Harris, a Black attorney whose offices were in Petersburg, but who lived in and represented Dinwiddie County in the General Assembly. A hostile lawsuit delayed opening day for nineteen months, until October 1, 1883. In 1902, the legislature revised the charter act to curtail the collegiate program and to change the name to Virginia Normal and Industrial Institute.

In 1920, the land- grant program for Blacks was moved from a private school, Hampton Institute, where it had been since 1872, to Virginia Normal and Industrial Institute. In 1923 the college program was restored.

The name was changed to Virginia State College for Negroes in 1930. The two-year branch in Norfolk was added to the college in 1944. The Norfolk division became a four-year branch in 1956 and gained independence as Norfolk State College in 1969. Meanwhile, the parent school was renamed Virginia State College in 1946. Years later, Virginia State College was changed Virginia State University in 1979 when the legislature in VA passed a law.

7 Ralph Johnson Bunche

Ralph Johnson Bunche who was born on August 7, 1903 in Detroit, Michigan. Bunche was a scholar, educator, civil rights advocate and world statesman. Bunche achieved international renown as the first person of color to receive the Nobel Peace Prize.

8 Parker-Gray School

Parker-Gray Elementary School was built for African Americans. It was named for African American educators John F. Parker and Sarah J. Gray. It became a four-year high school in 1932. School moved to a new building on Madison Street in 1950. It became a middle school in 1965 during desegregation, and closed in 1979.

9 George Washington High School

George Washington High School opened in the fall of 1935 at 1005 Mount Vernon Avenue, Alexandria, Virginia, merging the students from Alexandria's two high schools. GW, as it was popularly known, replaced Alexandria High School, which had been located in the 1400 block of Cameron Street, adjacent to Jefferson Elementary School. GW also replaced the George Mason High School, which was built in 1925 in the town of Potomac (formed in 1908 when Del Ray joined St. Elmo). In 1930, Alexandria annexed this town and also acquired the high school, which fronted 2500 Mount Vernon Avenue. Located adjacent to George Mason was Mt. Vernon Elementary School. With the opening of GW, George Mason High School became an annex to the nearby elementary school. The original George Mason High School building still stands as part of Mt. Vernon Elementary. All of these high schools served the white population of Alexandria, as segregation was the law in Virginia until after the 1954 Supreme Court decision. Parker-Gray High School on Madison Street served Alexandria's black population until 1965 when integration came to the city's high schools.

GW's original main building, built in the distinctive art deco style with exterior ornamental carved stonework and vertically fluted stone columns, was a three-story T-shape with one long hallway on each floor, stretching the length of the front of the building. There were no south or north wings in 1935. On the first floor, extending from the center of the rear of the school, were the locker rooms for boys and girls, with a long hallway in between leading to the cafeteria. On the second floor above the locker rooms was the auditorium, distinctive and unique at the time and built with such good acoustics that, in the early decades it was used for performances by the National Symphony Orchestra and professional opera companies; it was also mentioned in the Virginia history books. Also on the second floor, located above the cafeteria, was the gymnasium, which, though small, was a great improvement over the gym facilities of the former Alexandria and George Mason High Schools. The gym also served the band and became known to many as the band room.

The first principal of GW was Henry T. Moncure. His tenure began with a student body of approximately 1200 and a faculty of 35. At this time, both the School Board and Superintendent T.C. Williams were openly criticized for having built a school so large that, it was claimed, there would never be a student body large enough to use the entire facility. Three expansions of the building in less than ten years proved the critics' assessment to be completely off the mark.

The first expansion came in 1937, just two years after the school opened. This was the addition of the south wing that was used for shop classes. By 1941, a full industrial arts annex was constructed separate from the main building, across the parking lot from south entrance of the high school. In 1948 the north wing was built, providing more classrooms and housing the library on the third floor, with an extension to the cafeteria on the first floor. Room 108 was part of this expansion, and according to reports from teachers at the time, was to be used for meetings of professional educational clubs and associations, which justified outfitting the room with wood paneling, benches and a wet bar.

The GW Memorial Stadium, with a capacity of 14,800 fans, was built by the city in 1947, with merchants' donations funding the cost of the lights and a single corporation providing for the electronic scoreboard. The stadium, with its quarter-mile track and lighted football field, was often the site of professional preseason football games, three-ring

circuses, visits by U.S. Presidents, and every Thanksgiving
Day it was filled to capacity for the Olde Oaken Bucket
football game between GW and arch-rival Washington & Lee
High School of Arlington.

The small gymnasium was satisfactory during GW's early
years, but due to increased attendance at the varsity basketball
games, the gym facilities became inadequate. GW began to
play their home basketball games at Hammond High School
when it opened in 1956. After a long period of planning by
the city, the Tulloch Memorial Gymnasium was finally built,
opening in 1961. The old gymnasium was officially converted
into two music rooms and the locker rooms were made into
four classrooms.

After Alexandria's 1953 annexation of a large portion of
Fairfax County to the west of the city, additional students came
into the city school system, changing the demographics and
necessitating the planning and construction of another high
school. In 1956 Francis C. Hammond High School on
Seminary Road was opened, taking students from GW's
freshman and sophomore classes. The last class to graduate
intact from GW was the Class of 1957. The Class of 1958
was the first class to have its members, who were all at GW
for their freshman and sophomore years, graduate as a divided
class from GW and Hammond. The Class of 1959 also
graduated with its members divided between the two high
schools, after beginning as a unified freshman class at GW.

In the 1960s the City of Alexandria began planning for the
integration of the public schools. In 1965 T. C. Williams High
School was opened. GW was integrated and remained a 4-

year high school until 1971 when Alexandria's secondary schools were reorganized. At that time, both GW and Hammond were designated to serve ninth and tenth graders, while T. C. Williams was designated the city's senior high school. In 1979, the city again reorganized the secondary schools, and GW's status changed to a junior high. GW finally became a middle school in 1993, educating students in grades six through eight. This remains GW's mission in 1998.

10 Francis C. Hammond High School

Francis Colton Hammond was born November 9, 1931, in Alexandria, Virginia, the son of Harry C. Hammond and Elvira Jenkins Hammond.While still in high school, Francis Hammond worked for his future father-in-law's construction company and played guitar in a band, performing at local events. After graduating from George Washington High School in Alexandria, he worked with his father at Timberman's Pharmacy, an Alexandria landmark owned by his uncle. Although planning to become a pharmacist, Francis Hammond decided to join the Navy on March 20, 1951. With the realization that he would soon be shipped out to Korea, he requested and was granted permission to marry his high school sweetheart, Phyllis Ann Jenkins on June 19, 1952.

Hospitalman Francis Hammond received his orders to Korea and arrived there on February 1, 1953. After heroic efforts to assist his fallen comrades and refusing orders to withdraw even though wounded, Francis Hammond was killed in action on March 27, 1953, two weeks prior to his scheduled rotation out of the combat area. His son, Francis C. Hammond, Jr., was born seven months later. Hospitalman Francis Colton

Hammond was laid to rest with full military honors in Arlington National Cemetery. The Medal of Honor was presented to his wife and infant son on December 30, 1953. Francis C. Hammond High School was dedicated in 1956.

11 T.C. Williams High School

T.C. Williams is one of the most respected, comprehensive high schools in the country. Its facilities and its top students compare favorably with the best private schools. With a "going to college" rate of 84%, students from the class of 2000 have been admitted to more than 100 colleges and universities.

T.C. Williams is named for a former superintendent of schools who served from the mid-1930s until the mid-1960s. The school opened in 1965 and has served the Alexandria community and tens of thousands of students well for the past 33 years.

12 Jim Crow

Jim Crow was an antebellum character in a minstrel show. A white man (Tom "Daddy" Rice)- made up as a black man - incorporated a character called "Jim Crow" into his show in 1832. Jim Crow sang a song to this music "Weel about and turn about And do jis so, Eb'ry time I weel about And jump Jim Crow." Soon the term "Jim Crow" became a euphemism for "Negro." Soon the term "Jim Crow Laws" became a euphemism for legal segregation.

13 Brown v. Board of Education of Topeka (Brown I), 347 U.S. 483 (1954)

FACTS:
Four separate cases from the states of Kansas, South Carolina, Virginia, and Delaware were consolidated and decided in this case. In each of these cases, black children were denied admission to state public schools attended by white children under state laws requiring or permitting segregation according to race. There were findings that the black and white schools involved had been equalized, or were being equalized, with respect to buildings, curricula, qualifications and salaries of teachers, and other tangible factors. The legal representatives of the black children contend that segregated public schools are not "equal" and cannot be made "equal," and that hence they are deprived of the equal protection of the laws.

DECISION:
Segregation of white and Negro children in the public schools of a State solely on the basis of race, pursuant to state laws permitting or requiring such segregation, denies to Negro children the equal protection of the laws guaranteed by the Fourteenth Amendment — even though the physical facilities and other "tangible" factors of white and Negro schools may be equal.

(a) The history of the Fourteenth Amendment is inconclusive as to its intended effect on public education.
(b) The question presented in these cases must be determined, not on the basis of conditions existing when the Fourteenth Amendment was adopted, but in the light of the full development of public education and its present place in American life throughout the Nation.

(c) Where a State has undertaken to provide an opportunity for an education in its public schools, such an opportunity is a right that must be made available to all on equal terms.

(d) Segregation of children in public schools solely on the basis of race deprives children of the minority group of equal educational opportunities, even though the physical facilities and other "tangible" factors may be equal.

(e) The "separate but equal" doctrine adopted in Plessy v. Ferguson , 163 U.S. 537, has no place in the field of public education

(f) The cases are restored to the docket for further argument on specified questions relating to the forms of the decrees.

Brown v. Board of Education of Topeka (Brown II), 349 U.S. 294 (1955)

FACTS:
Brown I declared the fundamental principle that racial discrimination in public education is unconstitutional. All provisions of federal, state, or local law requiring or permitting such discrimination must yield to this principle. Because of the complexities involved in moving from a dual, segregated system to a unitary system of public education, the Court here considered the suggestions of the parties involved and of state and federal attorneys general.

The Court then returned the cases to the local federal courts, from which they had come, for action in accord with the guidelines below and with the Brown I decision.

DECISION:
1) Local school authorities have the primary responsibility

for implementing the Brown I decision. The function of the federal courts is to decide whether a school board is complying in good faith and to reconcile the public interest in orderly and effective transition to constitutional school systems with the constitutional requirements themselves.

2) However, the principle of equal educational opportunity cannot yield simply because of public disagreement. A "prompt and reasonable start" toward full compliance must be made, and compliance must proceed "with all deliberate speed."

Plessy vs. Ferguson

Plessy v. Ferguson , 163 U.S. 537 (1896)

FACTS:

A man who was a citizen of the United States and a resident of Louisiana challenged a Louisiana law that required railway corn-panics to provide separate-but-equal
facilities for whites and blacks and that provided criminal penalties for passengers who insisted on being seated in a car not reserved for their own race.

DECISION:

A law requiring segregation of the races in railway cars and providing for separate-but-equal facilities for both whites and blacks is constitutional.

1) The Thirteenth Amendment abolished slavery but is not a bar to actions, short of involuntary servitude, that nevertheless may burden the black race.

2) The Fourteenth Amendment prohibits the state from making any law that impairs the life, liberty, or property interest of

any person under the jurisdiction of the United States. Although this Amendment requires equality between the races before the law, it does not require the social commingling of the races or the abolition of social distinctions.

14 Swann vs. Charolette-Mecklenburg

In 1971 the Supreme Court ruling on the Swann vs. Charolette-Mecklenburg Board of Education case legitimized busing as a method to achieve desegregation.   In N.C., the General Assembly passed the Pupil Placement Act (1955). In Charlotte, a token integration occurred. In 1957, when a few black students were assigned to three white schools. In 1962, the Charlotte-Mecklenburg Board of Education adopted a plan of nonracial geographic assignment. The plan granted students the freedom to transfer from an area of black concentration. Some black schools were closed. With the passage of the Civil Rights Act of 1964, the Board faced a loss of federal funding unless the 1962 plan was revised to comply with federal policy on non-discrimination. As the Board began drawing up new plans, the class action suit James E. Swann, et al v. Charlotte-Mecklenburg Board of Education, was brought against them in January, 1965. The Board was charged with maintaining a segregated system. The suit was originated by Darius Swann, professor of theology at Johnson C. Smith University. Swann requested that his son James be allowed to attend the predominantly white school near their home instead of the predominantly black school some distance away. The Board denied his request. Subsequently his case and several others of a similar nature were brought to the court as a class action suit by the NAACP Legal Defense and Educational Fund through the services of Charlotte civil rights attorney Julius Chambers. The suit was brought before the U.S. District Court. There Judge J. Braxton Craven Jr. approved the Board's new plans for the 1965-66 school year.

The plaintiffs appealed the case to the Court of Appeals for the Fourth Circuit. Judge Clement Haynsworth upheld the District Court's ruling. The plaintiffs reopened the case in September, 1968, filing for further desegregation of the schools. Appointed to hear the case in the District Court was James B. McMillan Jr. Attorneys for the defendants were Brock Barkley, William J. Waggoner, and Benjamin S. Horack.

In April, 1969, McMillan ruled that there still existed a dual system in which schools were racially identifiable. He stated that discriminatory property laws, the "freedom of choice" clause, gerrymandering of district lines, and the "neighborhood school" theory were perpetrating segregated schools. Also, that the achievement scores of blacks in black schools were unacceptably low. In June, 1969, the Board submitted a plan that closed some black inner-city schools. These pupils were reassigned, along with other black students, to white schools.

In August, 1969, the court approved the implementation of this plan for the 1969-70 year. The Board was ordered to prepare by November a plan for desegregation according to balanced racial ratios. The Board's plan, submitted November 17, 1969, was not accepted by the Court because it continued to focus on freedom of choice and rezoning. In December, McMillan laid out specific guidelines for the preparation of plans that would desegregate the schools. Dr. John A. Finger, an educational consultant from Rhode Island College, was hired and instructed to prepare a plan that would reach to

improve the black to ratio in all schools. The goal was a ratio
of 71:29 whites to blacks.   The Board also prepared
desegregation plans. Both Finger and the Board prepared
separate plans for each level: high school, junior high, and
elementary. Both sets of plans were submitted to the Court in
February, 1970. Finger's plan relied substantially on busing.
McMillan subsequently rejected the Board's plans and ordered
the implementation of Finger's plans. Concurrently, as the
central issue was in the courts, supplementary suits were also
developing. In June, 1969, the N.C.General Assembly passed
an anti-busing statute. When the Charlotte-Mecklenburg
Board of Education was ordered in February,1970 to begin
busing, the N.C. Board of Education and several others sued
the Charlotte-Mecklenburg Board of Education. William Self,
superintendent of the Charlotte-Mecklenburg Schools was also
included in the suit. The cases, decided in Mecklenburg
County Superior Court, enforced a temporary restraining order
based on the use of public funds for busing in the desegregation
plan. These were ruled to be in conflict with the anti-busing
statute. The Swann plaintiffs moved to add these individuals
and the state as additional parties-defendant to prevent them
from interfering with federal court mandates. In March, 1970,
McMillan ordered that a three-judge court convene to rule on
the anti-busing statute. The three-judge court, presided over
by Circuit Court judges J. Braxton Craven and John Butzner,
and McMillan, District judge, ruled the anti-busing statute
unconstitutional. The N.C. State Board of Education and the
additional parties appealed the case to the Supreme Court.
Meanwhile, the central Swann case was on appeal in the
Fourth Circuit Court of Appeals. On May 26, 1970, the U.S.
Court of Appeals for the Fourth Circuit, approving most of
the Finger plan dealing with the junior and senior high schools.

The part that applied to elementary schools that provided for additional busing of several thousand elementary school children to achieve a racial balance in schools that would otherwise be predominantly black or white was rejected. The basis for the judges' ruling was the opinion that every school does not need to be integrated under a unitary system, particularly when such integration would require extreme cross-busing. The primary consideration to be applied in deciding local cases is the "test of reasonableness." The elementary plan was remanded back to the District Court for redrafting. McMillan ordered that the U.S. Department of Health, Education, and Welfare assist in the preparation of new elementary school plans. When the case was appealed to the U.S. Supreme Court, the issue was whether school boards were required to use all available means to achieve integration. The Board of Education also filed a motion to stay the implementation of the Finger and HEW plans for the 1970-71 school year.

The Supreme Court agreed to hear the case in October, 1970. A stay was of the District Court's order was refused. Instead, on June 29, 1970, the Supreme Court mandated that the orders of the District Court be reinstated for the 1970-71 school year for all grade levels. Mass busing of students began that year. In April, 1971, the Supreme Court ruled that the Finger Plan was a constitutional method for desegregating high school, junior high, and elementary level grades. Thus the District Court's original ruling of February, 1970 was upheld.

The implications of the decision were that all available means must be used to desegregate the schools. Busing as a means to achieve racial desegregation is constitutional. Following

the Supreme Court's decision, the District Court was charged
with ensuring that adequate desegregation plans continued to
be implemented in the Charlotte-Mecklenburg schools. After
the Swann case authorized busing to speed up the integration
process, in 1971, the city of Alexandria found itself under
pressure to come up with a plan to integrate all schools. The
integration had to be in proportion to the racial mix of the
student population.

15 Titan

The word Titan comes from an account in Greek mythology.
The Titans were a family of giants born of Uranus and Gaea
and ruling the earth until overthrown by the Olympian god.

Index

S

T

V

W

Y

Bibliography

Info regarding Remember the Titans and Jim Crow" Laws
www.awesomestories.com/history

Summaries of the US Supreme Court Decisions done by
Loucas Petronicolos as listed on www.uwosh.edu/
faculty_staff/petronic

Information from the official T.C.Williams High School
Website at www.acps.k12.va.us/profiles/tcwilliams.html

Historical information about the City of Alexandria from
the Web Site at http://ci.alexandria.va.us/city/timeline

Information on George Washington High School from
http://gwaa.acps.k12.va.us/history.html

Information on Virginia State University from
www.vsu.edu website

Information on Norfolk State University from
www.nsu.edu website.

Information on the Norfolk Navy Shipyard from
www.nnsy1.navy.mil/History

Information on Booker T. Washington High on
www.nps.k12.va.us/schools/btw/history.htm.

Support the 71 Original Titans Foundation Scholarship Fund

The Titan Foundation was established by the coaches, players, and cheerleaders from the 1971 Virginia AAA State Champion Varsity Football Team of T. C. Williams High School. The Foundation is a nonprofit organization dedicated to helping high school students pursue post-secondary education. As a named scholarship of the Scholarship Fund of Alexandria, the Foundation provides educational support to eligible seniors from T.C. Williams High School in the form of a renewable grant for four years. Post-secondary education is critical to the development and growth of our community. Many students have the potential to excel academically, but lack the resources to pursue higher education. Providing this support the Titan Foundation is helping the community grow through the better education of its young people.

How to Make a Contribution:

Make Check payable to the '71 Original Titans' and mail it to:

'71 Original Titans
P. O. Box 23371
Alexandria, Virginia 22304
Visit www.71originaltitans.com for more information.

To contact the Alexandria Scholarship Fund:
Visit www.alexscholarshipfund.org

The Scholarship Fund of Alexandria is a fund of The
Community Foundation for the National Capital Region, I
private nonprofit, 501(c)(3), charitable organization. The Titan
Foundation is a private nonprofit, 501(c)(3), charitable
organization. Current financial statements are available
through the Scholarship Fund or the Titan Foundation

Hiya Sis, I still have a warm feeling from seeing Coach..No
one will ever know what a huge influence He had on Me...He
and His family have been in My prayers for along time... I
wish they had shown the trip to semi-state when the bus broke
down and We all had to pile into one bus...and My teammates
made sure everyone of the 'starters' had a seat...We never
looked at the color of a kids skin only if He was the best
player for that position..maybe I was young and dumb but
when I met your father I didn't see a 'black man' I saw a
'Man' that thru His faith in Me made Me a better player and a
better Man.....I tested His faith severely but I always knew
He was there and the Lord blessed Me when He brought Him
into My life...and if the Foundation puts just one child into
college it is all worth it...Your Friend Always, **Dan Carl**

Acknowledgments

Acknowledgements and thanks go to the following:

Loucas Petronicolos for giving permission to use a summary of information he compiled regarding the summary of the Supreme Court decisions.

Lee Wood for giving me your time and attention (and correction) enabling me to finish this project.

Ramona Toliver for reading the manuscript early on when the mistakes were overwhelming and for keeping it a secret.

Daniel Lonergan for letting me be me, crazy and free and loving me despite myself.

Catherine Lonergan for reading the manuscript in its early stages.

Jami Hill for your reading at the toward the end.

George T. for your wonderful foreward.

Bobbie Christensen for the seminar and guidance that encouraged me to finish this project.

Grandpa and Grandma Toliver for providing me with little tidbits and insights along the way for it helped me to put this story together.

Joseph Toliver for telling me about schooling at Ralph Bunche, the outhouses, and bus rides.

The Hill-Williams family for many fun and happy reunions memories, which are still etched in my mind.

Leland and Pearl Hines for being my straightforward and fun-loving uncle and aunt.

Mike for being a brother who still plays and jokes with me as if we were still children, even though we have long since been grown.

Greg Hiscott of California Key Connections for the web support, and introducing me to web designing. (A heads up to my buddy Derek)

Thanks to Carole Bos at Lawbuzz.com for permission to use excerpts from a few of her awesomestories.com web pages.

Carmelita Hearn for your willingness to read the manuscript and finding it delightful.

The City of Alexandria Web Team for permission to use the City Timeline.

Belinda Belisle for the information at the editing and proofreading class, which showed me all the things I was doing wrong and for reviewing the manuscript.

Ted Arthur and Marty Neely for permission to use the information on the G.W. High School web site.

Kassy Benson for permission to use the information about Hammond even though this project relates to T.C. (you were right!)

Thanks to the 71 Titans who contributed their personal thoughts to Doc.

A thank you to all my family who have loved me all my life.

A thank you to my friends who have supported and encouraged me all my life.

Thanks to all the people who have supported all my websites and provided feedback (good and bad), whether via email or on the guestbook.

To all of the Titans thanks for all years and games and loving my father.

And to the 71 Titans, thanks for your wonderful example and making me an honorary member.

If I have omitted anyone, please know it is a mistake of the head, not the heart.

Special Acknowledgment

Behind every good man is a good woman. In the case of you, mommy, you are not only a good wife, but a good mother. You have always made Daddy look good. Mommy, the movie wasn't specifically about you, but you are a backbone and an important key to the real life story of Daddy.

You were firm when I needed it, even though I didn't like it. You taught me the important things, even though I didn't know the things were important at the time. You were steadfast when my youthful world was insecure and unsure. You didn't give up on me and kept working with me, never giving up. You remained consistent and scheduled, keeping first things first and fun things in their place. You have remained tenacious in setting a fine example and keeping your faith strong.

Gracious for everything...

About the Author

Paula Hines Lonergan resides in Pasadena, California, with her husband, Daniel, and her cat, Fraidi. She is a big fan of her father Paul "Doc" Hines. She has cheered for T.C. Williams High School since she was a little girl. She works at the California Institute of Technology and is involved in a volunteer ministry work. She does web designing and freelance writing.

To Order A Titan of a Man

A Titan of a Man
ISBN: **0-9743957-0-6**   **Price: $12.50**

To Order by Mail:
If ordering via mail, please complete the order form and mail it with remittance to the address provided on the next page.

To order by Telephone (Call Toll-Free)
With Master Card or Visa only, call 1-800-929-7889

To order online, go to:
www.ATitanofaMan.com

To Order A Titan of a Man

A Titan of a Man
ISBN: 0-9743957-0-6   **Price: 12.50**

Quantity of Books	Unit Price	Total

Subtotal $_____
8.25% Sales Tax (CA only) $_____
Shipping and Handling * $_____
Total Order $_____

---

*Shipping and Handling depends on the number of books ordered.
  See below:
1 Book - $2.95   2-5 Books - $5.95   6-10 Books - $9.95
For orders over 10 books, please contact publisher.

Just fill out the information below and send this page with your
remittance to:
PRL PUBLISHING, Order Department
Attention: Paula Lonergan
2245 E. Colorado Boulevard, No. 104 PMB 243
Pasadena, CA 91107

— —

Name _____

Address _____

City _____State _____Zip _____

Daytime Phone _____

Email address
(optional) _____
Check/Money Order (US drawn only) enclosed for $_____